ALL THINGS

— ARE —

FULFILLED

ALL THINGS
— *ARE* —
FULFILLED

THE KEY TO LIVING THE LIFE OF YOUR
DREAMS IS NOT WHAT YOU THINK....
IT'S WHAT YOU KNOW

PATRICK STILLWELL

HIGHERLIFE
PUBLISHING & MARKETING
Oviedo, Florida

CONTENTS

MY STORY

I WROTE THIS BOOK BECAUSE I want people to know about Jesus Christ. I know most people have heard of Jesus and most people will say they have been to church. I wrote this book in the hope that people would take *another look* at Jesus and see Him like never before! This has been my desire since May 21, 1991, when God opened my eyes to see that Jesus was more than I thought He was. At that time, I started telling everyone I could about Him. What I discovered was that almost everyone I talked with said they knew Jesus and they were Christians or that they went to church.

In this book I want to share my transition from seeking God's supernatural miracles for needs in my life, to seeking Him personally, just to know Him. I want to convey the peace and stability this brought to my life and also the enormous resistance to this process of knowing God, both internal, within myself, and external, from forces without.

My hope is that in this book called *All Things Are Fulfilled*, God will open hearts to see the simplicity of His plan and the benefits of knowing Him personally. Through knowing God personally, a person can more readily discern His voice and, with high confidence and trust, follow God's advice for their life. When we find ourselves not able to trust our normal ways of obtaining information, we will see that He has given us a more sure way of knowing and communicating than we ever had, or perhaps needed. When a person knows God, they can be more sure and certain that they are led by their "God feeling" rather than their "gut feeling," causing satisfaction to abound!

The main culprit of deception is the corrupted flesh we live in. Our carnal body has a deep hatred toward God, so our spirit is constantly redirected toward a wrong path. This book will expose this, but we must be aware that our own mind and heart and natural desires will fight God's Word and Spirit, taking over leadership in our life. Our own carnal mind will feed us a lying thought to retain its stronghold in our life. As we learn to discern and resist this evil, we grow in confidence and trust in the word of truth, allowing God's unlimited power to work through us.

ENJOY!

Pat Stillwell

INTRODUCTION

HAVE YOU EVER WONDERED WHY at the front of a book there will be an "Introduction?" Then furthermore you'll find a "Foreword," and sometimes a "Prologue?" I'm thinking, "Don't you just need one of these?" Sometimes when I'm picking up a book to read, I will want to go right to the main body of the book because I'm so interested in the subject, but most of the time I want to know where the writer is coming from. I'm usually curious about what made a person want to believe what they are writing about. I strongly suggest to any person taking a look at this book that you read all three, for if your heart is not pricked by these opening words, your mind may not be open to the thoughts that are presented. You see, the primary reason I wrote this book is the hope that all people could receive the encouragement and motivation to desire to know the fulfillment of life on earth. That every person would know the way to have a consistent joy-filled life.

The fundamental irregularity that you will need to overcome to understand this book is my writing style. You see, early on, as I became aware that Jesus Christ is a person that we can actually get to know, I also realized that the ones teaching about Him all had different ideas of who He was. So this led me to the conclusion that if I went to any particular denominational Bible school I would have to be indoctrinated by their restricted understanding of who they say Jesus Christ is and what He is about. I knew this meant that I would be conditioned by what I was taught, rather than being led by what I felt in my heart was true. Understanding this also led me to the decision not to receive formal education in proper writing so as to not adversely impact what I was trying to convey. So my hope is that you can overlook my lack of proper English grammar and be excited about the almost unadulterated words of experience from the eyes of my innocence, learned by experience of sixty years of observations of life in Christ, both before and after I knew who He is.

THE SERPENT'S STRATEGY

This key of understanding opens the door of knowledge to the Father's blueprint design. Our Father in heaven is the cord that holds all humanity together. God has designed that Jesus is in a marriage relationship with redeemed mankind; men and women who trust in God and Christ are intended to be "Brides of Christ." So this relationship with Him allows us to persevere in marriage on earth, overcoming all dark attacks against the family, and experience the greatest love.

This allows us to know His love for us far more and appreciate the sacrifice of Jesus.

A man without knowledge and faith to hear from God our Father in heaven feels worthless, defeated, and discouraged because of his failures, and without encouragement believes the lies of the dark side and falls idle, or worse, succumbs to the accuser's barrage.

Marriage without the sanctified woman's prayers for her man and without the man subject to the Word, which is Christ (John 1:1, 14), tends toward confusion. At times the hatred of the deceived or unsanctified woman toward the man who is deceived or not subject to the Word grows stronger as each day passes (Ephesians 5:23–24). So the woman waits for the man to get right as she takes on more and more responsibility in life, ever increasing her stress, pain, and anger focused toward the failure of the man. Now her frustrations are turned to enmity toward the man because it is so naturally obvious that he is at fault. The focus of her hostility is toward the man rather than the darkness that has overwhelmed them both.

The woman expects the children to give her comfort. However, the daughter is drawn to find a man and torn, knowing her mom needs love and that she can't fulfill that need. The son, without access to the Father in heaven, feels lost and confused. Without an earthly father to point him to his Heavenly Father's voice, the son rejects his responsibilities as a man.

All the while the hordes of darkness are in raunchiest celebration, anticipating complete control of mankind. As the dark armies nervously await the outcome of their bargain for desires, God the Father patiently awaits, moving into position His last days special forces. As they seek to know Him better today than they did yesterday, they will recognize His voice when He calls. This book is written to these special forces of God.

So, right now, troops of light, grab hold of the Word of God and write it upon your heart. Then, when the voice of our Father in heaven sounds, we will be familiar with it. We'll have learned to obey by faith the direction of light that agrees with the principle of the Word we know so well. With joy and confidence we anticipate the command of God! (Jeremiah 31:33–34).

KNOWLEDGE IN THE NIGHT

One morning, God awoke me with some understanding. At 7:01 a.m. I got up to write what the Lord was instructing me that day. The Holy Ghost was talking to me at first about how He brought me to my beautiful wife who was full of faith in God and His Son Jesus Christ. Of course, at that time in my life I didn't know how to define faith, except by observing a person's life. If they were nice, didn't cuss or drink much, and did the responsible things in their life, they must be Christians, or people of faith. So my wife was this kind of woman when we met in our early twenties. I was very impressed by how much intense pressure she was under, and yet she did her duty, her responsibility, taking care of her son, having no father to help, except her own father.

As I lay on my bed listening, I understood that God was showing me the examples in my life that helped bring about the finished work He had me write in this book entitled *All Things Are Fulfilled*. I realized that He was showing me that both my wife Carol and I were like so many people. We were conditioned to believe a certain way but hadn't come to the fullness of life that God intended. I was listening to the Lord on my bed that morning as the Holy Ghost instructed. I started to see the whole picture of how the things He allowed in my life pertained to an overview of this book's Spirit-inspired message.

So God's fulfillment of life for us, His desire, is that we would know Him, love to be around Him, and actually desire to do what He wants. In other words, trust His voice, His command, His direction above our logical comprehension. He wants a people like Jesus, who only depended on what His Father in heaven said, and responded in obedience when He saw what His Father wanted Him to do (John 2:24–25; John 5:19, 30). God desires a people who place faith in their knowledge of God above their ability to understand the fullness of what God is accomplishing, a people who could recognize His voice and obey His command. So my experience of knowing God that morning began with a review of what I already knew: the Lord brought my wife and me together to show that my logic without faith in God was limited and my wife's faith without complete knowledge of Scripture was limited. However, faith coupled with the complete knowledge of Scripture affords the opportunity to believe two vital things. First, we can hear God's command from heaven today and second, we can believe by faith what can't be explained and understood by logic alone (Revelation 4:1; 22:14).

So the Lord continued that morning by using the example of the many people I have met and known through my sixty years of life. He caused me to see in an instant all the different cases demonstrating life led by great faith, little faith, no faith, anti-faith, and evil. The Holy Ghost said that these were examples of people who were living either by their own direction or by the direction of God. The fact is that if we reject a written document to follow, we will still be following something. It may be the whim of the loudest voice seeming to point to the most beneficial path. The Lord taught further, "It's like they have put a king in charge of their life, but he is a puppet king; he has no authority. For without an unchanging principled written document to follow, we will be persuaded by whatever sounds best at that time." The Lord continued, "So the majority of My creation believe either they are in control of their life, or I am, but they are wrong. You see, most of My creation follows a voice or gut feeling they cannot identify with personal knowledge of My written Word. As a result, they are actually in confusion and living in unrest." The Lord showed seven examples of the way people live, two groups having no confessed belief in God, five with confessed belief in God. Yet only one group actually loved God enough to seek to know Him by reading His Word and placing it in their heart. This one group had developed their confidence, or faith, or courage, in Him alone. They had the boldness to step out and live by faith in the voice of God alone without the limiting agreement of their logical understanding. They were led by God alone, not by their own senses or by the will of the greatest majority.

After this, the Lord instructed further. "The fulfillment of My desire for My people is for them to trust fully in me, not as My original disciples did, but as Jesus did. Become My sons and daughters, My children, the seed of My only begotten Son, Jesus Christ (Isaiah 53:10; John 8:29). The battle My people face is the resistance of the corrupted flesh" (Romans 8:5–7). The Spirit of Christ more perfectly directs us by the written Word of God. This Word must be engraved in the fleshly heart in order to restrain the willful desires of the corrupted flesh. Resisting the flesh takes great labor, but the end produced is a "haven of rest" on earth for God's people (Hebrews 4:9, 11). God speaks to each one of us: "Rewrite your preconditioned mind to My way, My Word, and begin the new life in Me, becoming a friend of Jesus Christ." We are perfected in Christ as we believe the Lord's instinct, the God feeling in us, the way we believe our own instinct, our natural gut feeling. This is perfection in Christ.

UNPLANNED

If ever there was something I did not want to do, it is what I believe the Lord woke me up that morning and told me to do. Understand, I believe I am in the Army of God and when He instructs, my duty is to obey. He told me to write these thoughts and use them as the beginning of this book called *All Things Are Fulfilled.*

I had just seen the movie *Unplanned*, which had come out in the theaters that weekend (3-30-2019). The movie depicted the abortion industry in America, using events in the life of one person who was involved with a Planned Parenthood Clinic in Houston, Texas. I experienced a mix of emotions during and after the movie and even as I awoke, the strongest feeling dominating me was an overwhelming emptiness, perhaps better described as deadness. I don't know why exactly I felt this way, but I would emphasize an important point about the feeling. God was using this experience and emotion to prepare me to do my duty, even as a soldier is trained and prepares for war and is made ready and willing to go to battle. So with both excitement and the sense of danger it felt like I was being ushered into what I have been prepared for, and I'm thankful for that.

The movie depicted in a specific series of events the details of how the devil uses good-hearted people to accomplish his work. His strategies could only come from centuries of prior experience. This is why I had the feeling of deadness, because without the known protection and guidance of the

Lord, I would be way over my head coming into battle with the arch-enemy of our soul. Here are the principles that I noticed in the film. I will list them as they come to mind:

1. First, what stands out is the biblical principle that is summarized, "wherever two or three or more witnesses agree is truth" (Deut. 17:6). It seems clear that humans are put together in such a way that this principle works for either good or bad, emphasizing the grave need to read, know, and do what the Bible tells us is right and true.

2. Second, what we focus on is what we will do, especially if we believe what we are doing is good and right and true (Matthew 6:22–23).

3. Third, neither logic nor love can always change an engraved heart immediately, demonstrating that impressions engraved on the heart are dominant over both intelligence and compassion. Understand that logic and love are very important and key to the human experience, but what is engraved on our hearts, our conditioning, can only be changed through patience over time (Jeremiah 31:33). This is evidence of and proves the wisdom of God's command to wait with patience as He works by His Spirit and Word to open people's hearts to His truth. For believers in God, being patient is a key element in our preparation to be His servants, and is mentioned seven times in the book of Revelation (Revelation 1:9; Revelation 2:2–3, 19; Revelation 3:10; Revelation 13:10; Revelation 14:12).

4. Fourth, it is very apparent that the devil uses his influence to put people in high, powerful positions. Then they can put into places of authority those of like mind and heart, led by one possessing the gift of charisma. Satan's sole purpose in doing this is to control and destroy life (Ephesians 6:12). The dark side's primary desire is to control and conquer humans. The Bible uses the term "Nicolaitans," derived from "to conquer the Laodicean, or to be victorious over the lay people." This term is used by Jesus to say He hates the deeds of them, the Nicolaitans (Revelation 2: 6, 15). The church of the city of Laodicea is the last of the seven churches warned in the Bible. Jesus rebukes this church for being lukewarm but reminds them that He stands at the door of the heart and knocks (Revelation 3:16, 20).

This is the basic template of the devil's plan to overcome and control and destroy God's creation. This book presents the "how to" for victory over the attack of our enemy, by knowing the voice of God.

PREFACE

THE JOURNEY, A SHIP ON THE SEA

WHEN YOU KNOW GOD, YOU know the Bible, and you recognize His voice (1 John 2:3–4). He will speak at what seems like the most unusual times.

One day as I was working in my business, vacuuming a pool, the Holy Ghost began to teach, saying, "The sailing ship is like the church of Jesus Christ on the earth. As the ship is the safest place to be in the middle of the storm in the sea, so you are safest as you prepare yourself to be a living tabernacle, the vessel, ark, or ship of the Lord, so that when you encounter storms on the sea of this life on earth, if you abide, stay, dwell in Me and I in you, you can trust that you rest safely with Me" (John 14:10–15, 20–24). For if the living Spirit, the Holy Ghost, and the sword of the Spirit, the written Word, abide in you, then you stay safe. As we all have our part as the so-to-speak crew on this ship called the church on earth (Romans 12:4–5), so we need to be perfect in Christ

(Ephesians 4:13) in order to have His direction from His throne in heaven.

This book is actually a compilation of certain events I have encountered during my time on this sea of life on earth. I have become aware, or at least inwardly sensible, that these events concern the authenticity of God and Jesus Christ. The book follows the course of time and events that I encountered as I've sought to convey to people how this amazing guy named Jesus did these great things in my life.

One of the first things I became aware of was that people really wanted to know the story of the great acts God had performed in my life. They would tear up, laugh, they would listen intently, but then they would say they already believed in God, or went to church and that would be the end. Some people had a bad experience with church or life in general and had given up trying to believe God would actually do something really amazing just for them. The typical feeling I came away with was that they had lost hope. Through these two conflicting responses, joy, then hopelessness, God began to draw me to ask, "Why?" This lure of "Why?" built a great drawing power within me that remains and has grown stronger over the years. I believe that drawing power is the Holy Spirit of God calling me to His work.

The problem was plain to see. But the answer, although simple, was hidden under layers and layers and layers of deception. The deception was not only outside from other people and institutions but also inside myself. The elaborate complexity of duplicity was daunting, but at the same time the amount of effort it took to build such entanglement of confusion caused me to think that something really good must be buried beneath it. I was compelled toward the great prize just waiting to be uncovered. That is the purpose of this book, *All Things Are Fulfilled*. The answer is simple. The answer is to know the Word of God so that a person can discern the Spirit of God when He speaks, then simply do what He says. The simple answer is made difficult by the great resistance we need to overcome. In this book is the "how to," the tools I have used, the successes, and the setbacks. I hope you will come on board this ship, which could be called the Ark of God, so that you may find the fulfillment of hope for your life too.

The Ark of the Covenant, also called the Ark of the Testimony, is a rectangular box kept in the most sacred place in the temporary tabernacle designed by God and built by Moses. The Ark held the Ten Commandments (the Law of God), the manna (the bread that came from heaven), and the rod of Aaron that budded (the miraculous sign from God that Aaron was to be a priest of God). Through Jesus Christ believers are to be the Ark of God's power on earth.

The core of *All Things Are Fulfilled* is that God has been developing some things through the ages that required centuries to mature, but now today, across the world and especially in America, these actions are in the final stage of completion. They are being fulfilled, and simultaneously challenged.

The desire of God is simple, fellowship, but the obstacle is darkness, corruption, ignorance. In order to fellowship with

God, we must walk in the light (1 John 1:6–7). We must be illuminated by the truth of Jesus Christ and know the Bible, rather than become a deceptive counterfeit of what someone told us it means to be a Christian. After Jesus' sacrifice is revealed to us personally as payment for our sin, we can achieve fulfillment by immersing ourselves in the Word of God, the Bible. We must read it and know it to properly recognize God's voice. Then we need to practice changing our idea of what is good and bad, then condition ourselves until hearing the voice of God and obeying becomes habit. This is the fulfillment of the central objective of God's plan for man and the earth: fellowship with His creation throughout all the earth. His desire is to love us and to have us desire to love Him.

WHAT'S THE OBJECTIVE?

If the serpent in the Garden of Eden had the ability to trick God and spoil the Almighty's plan for His divine will, could we truly call Him Sovereign God, or all-powerful God?

To know that a plan is fulfilled, we must first understand the objective. In general, the Christian Church seems to portray the objective as "Believe in God," but perhaps there is more. When seeking answers to difficult matters, humans characteristically look for the most knowledgeable person and ask them about the subject. This is problematic in trying to comprehend the God of the Bible simply because there are so many religions and factions of those religions. Since religions promote so many differing thoughts on who God is and what He is instructing us in His Bible, it seems the most sure way to know the objective of the Almighty is to read the book ourselves. Of course, not everyone can do this, but surely God intends those with access to the Bible to model His image and set an example for others. They should be able to point to the direction of God's goal for humanity.

God's number one goal seems to be His desire to fellowship with like-minded individuals, people who <u>freely</u> make the choice to know Him and to desire to be with Him and obey Him.

This is the difference between being called a servant or being called a friend. Do you want to know Him? He gave us the book that explains who He is. He desires us to know Him. He's reaching out to mankind in the way He believes is best. Do you love Him enough to spend the time to read His Book, so that you would know that you know Him? His other goal is to show His mercy and grace toward those whose hearts are truly desiring His will and not their own. People, not without fault, but hungering to know the way to go in this life. Lastly, when Jesus was asked about the fullness of time on earth in Matthew 24:15, He referred the disciples to the book of Daniel in the Old Testament, saying, "Let him who reads understand." In Daniel's book there is one reference (12:7) where God answers the question, "How long will it be till the end of these wonders?" (fulfillment of God's purpose). God replied, "When I have accomplished to scatter the power of the holy people, all these things shall be fulfilled." The power of the holy people is their faith in God, not their faith in groups of people. Thus, it seems God's purpose is to spread His Word and the power of His Spirit's communication to the ends of the earth, so that each nation, people, language, and kindred would have the free opportunity to make the decision to know and choose Him. Perhaps the fulfillment of all things is when the people on earth begin to pray Jesus' prayer given to us in Matthew 6:10, "Thy kingdom come." Possibly this will be the prayer of the saints which is offered on the altar of God in heaven, recorded in Revelation 8:4 just after the seventh seal is opened, which precipitates God's salvation coming from heaven to rescue believers on earth from the evil to come and to punish the wicked. This is one reason why the Jewish nation and/or the Roman authority at that time was given the power to slay the Son of God, so that the power of the holy people would spread.

Both Jews and Romans were blind at that time to God's plan. He was demonstrating God's great mercy, grace, and love toward all people by allowing His sin-free Son to be sacrificed for the sins of the world. Salvation was freely available if people would only believe (John 12:39–40; Isaiah 6:8–10). Jesus quoted Isaiah, saying, "He hath blinded their eyes and hardened their heart, that they should not see with their eyes, nor understand with their heart." God's chosen children, the Jews, were given the law of God and found they could not obey it all. So God's ultimate purpose seems to be to give all humanity the opportunity to know and trust in Him, to realize we can't figure it all out, and to desire to spend eternity in

His loving presence. So if you can read, study the old Jewish Book, as well as the Christian New Testament. Then, realizing you can only know God's character through knowledge of the Book, you can begin to recognize God's way, by faith obey the voice of His spirit, and be in peace (Ephesians 3:19; John 14:27).

A PICTURE OF PATIENCE

Perhaps the Apostle Paul (who was the converted Jewish Pharisee named Saul) was used to spread the message of Jesus Christ because of his mind's capacity and his education and experience with the Jewish religion and Roman government. This possibly gave him the ability to withstand the hardness of people's hearts and minds toward him. These people were hard because of their engraved knowledge of the wrongs Saul committed against Christians before his actual experience with Jesus Christ. Because Paul experienced God's patience toward him, he could be more tolerant as he waited on the Holy Ghost to open the minds and hearts of the people. Both Jews and Gentiles had to break open their hardened souls to receive the truth of Jesus Christ. Many times I see in myself and others a shortness of patience when a truth is revealed. We must realize there is a time and a period of acceptance of new ideas, a breaking of old habits that we believed as fact. It simply takes a great deal of time for humans to adjust … even when they realize a new truth. It is our nature to be creatures of habit.

PROLOGUE

GOD REVEALS HIS MYSTERIES
IN OUR STRUGGLES

It is not common knowledge that the book of Revelation was written after all the original apostles except John were killed, and John was in prison for his stand for Christ and the Word. In other words, what God gave to John, in the book of Revelation, was further information of what God's purpose was. That knowledge was not complete or fulfilled by what believers knew through the Old Testament, or understood by what the disciples wrote in the New Testament. Neither was it completely revealed by the Holy Spirit at that time. Added to knowledge of the Old and New Testaments, the book of Revelation gives complete understanding to the work that God is in the process of fulfilling. Completely fulfilled understanding won't even come till the blowing of the seventh trumpet by the seventh angel, written about in Revelation 10:7. The timing of that actual happening is clarified in Revelation 11:15 as occurring soon after the two witnesses are killed, resurrected, and carried to heaven out of the city of Jerusalem. The point here is that we can't understand certain things of God's plan and purpose at present. They are presently sealed from our eyes, but those who diligently seek to know Him will be rewarded. In Hebrews 11:6, believers are told "for he that cometh to God must believe that he is, and that he is a rewarder of them that diligently seek Him." The Old Testament prophet Jeremiah tells us in Jeremiah 29:13, "And ye shall seek me, and find me, when you search for me with all your heart." Finally, Jesus told His followers in Matthew 7:7–8 "Ask, and it shall be given you; seek, and ye shall find; knock, and it shall be opened unto you: for every one that asketh receiveth; and he that seeketh findeth; and to him that knocketh it shall be opened." So seek to know God so that His mysteries can be seen as He reveals them. This is worth the effort of the sacrifice of our time.

The things of God are revealed to those who seek to know God (Ephesians 3:5). The last fulfilling may be when all men realize it is safer to live by faith in God than to trust in the leadership of men. What hinders the advancement of our understanding of God's purpose on earth is the resistance of our corrupted habitual nature. This nature can only be properly reset by our knowledge of God's Word and the collaborating witness of the Holy Spirit, not just by attending church. The deception of what is commonly seen as Christianity, which is simply going to church, conceals the fact that the Christian's goal after believing Christ by faith is to know God, hear His voice, and then obey.

You have the choice of either spending the majority of your time making your living on earth, or of finding your life in God. This choice is the ongoing war being waged in our heart and soul (mind, will, emotions). The lack of understanding what God is accomplishing through our time on earth is the principle cause of the worldwide delusions that will usher in the evil leadership which will rule the earth (Revelation 13:7).

Spend the time to know the Bible, to know Him (John 1:1; John 1:14). Jesus is the breath of God, heard by man and written in the words of the Bible.

The issue is that for the most part God is not seen as real, so that gaining knowledge of the Bible would seem to be a waste of time. So the foundational facet of unbelief to overcome may be the lack of an actual experience with God. We need an event, something that is so far removed from our natural understanding that we are compelled to seek to know God in order to gain understanding.

It seems also that mass media has conditioned the world to trust an electronic device rather than to trust people. In our individual, personal, Christian relationships we should encourage each other in faith in God, so strengthening each other in the power of God. Instead, the mass media draws us away from each other and to itself, in order for their power to grow. The conditioning effect of mass media seems to also cause both believers and non-believers to doubt their ability to know and realize the truth of God by their own investigation. One of the ways this is evidenced is that most of what one hears about the book of Revelation is that Christians will be taken off the earth so that they will not suffer. Even Christ had to learn obedience by suffering (Hebrews 5:8). We are also told in the Bible that the suffering of this present time is not worthy to be compared to the glory which shall be revealed in us (Romans 8:18). Also, believers on earth are recorded in the last book all the way up to Revelation 18:4, just before the great evil power that rules the earth, Babylon, will be destroyed. There are only twenty-two chapters in the book of Revelation.

A key enigma presented by our conditioning without the Bible's guidelines is that we have been led to believe that if God were good, He would eradicate our suffering. Our time of suffering actually gives the opportunity for us to cut out the noisy voices and distractions around us and focus our attention on seeking to know and trust in eternity with God (Romans 8:18). The book of Revelation, the very book of the Bible that informs us of detailed descriptions of the very last days, tells us that those who believe in the Bible and Jesus Christ will suffer. Only three of the twenty-two chapters of the book of Revelation do not mention followers of Christ suffering.

One of the chief reasons Satan hates and makes war against the Jews is their knowledge and honor of the Word of God. One of the principle reasons Satan hates and makes war against the believers in Christ is that they know and honor the Spirit of God, the Spirit that dwelt in Jesus Christ, the Sprit that dwells in believers, the Holy Ghost (Revelation 12:17). When the Jew and Christian come together honoring their gifts, the two witnesses, this will be completion, fulfillment, the finish. The written Word of God is thus testified to by the living voice of God, giving direction and power of God to those who believe (Ephesians 4:10, 13). God will fill all things with His Spirit, bringing unity through Christ and creating the mature perfect man in Jesus. Romans 8:4 says the law is fulfilled in those who walk after the Spirit, not after the flesh.

The Spirit is not some far off, airy thing we can't know. Ephesians 6:17 tells us "the sword of the Spirit is the Word of God." So knowing the Bible allows a person to know the Spirit of God.

THE GOD OF COMFORT

One of the greatest ways God brings peace to His children is to speak to us in ways that comfort. This is what this book will show you; this is what God did for me and what He wants to do for all who desire to hear His voice and obey. Here is one instance of His instruction to me which started sixteen years ago and is the basis of God's method of fulfilling.

The Lord instructed me years ago through the book of Ephesians: "I will show you your vocation." At that time I was only given the unique meaning of the word "vocation" as used in Ephesians 4:1 to be incited, urged by the Spirit of

God. The Lord taught later that the incitement of the Holy Spirit tells us when to act and the insight of the Holy Spirit tells us how to act. As Jesus said about Himself, I only do and say what I hear and see the Father doing (John 5:19, 30). This morning as I lay in bed, the Lord took me chapter by chapter through the book of Ephesians and said very concisely what each chapter had to say and do with His vocation for me.

He showed me how hearing His voice and seeing His plan fulfills His purpose on earth. That purpose is to bring forth or birth many servant/friends of God who will rule and reign with Him and Christ for their thousand-year reign on earth (Revelation 20:4). This morning the Lord elaborated on how the word "vocation" (meaning incitement of the Holy Spirit), used in Ephesians 4:1, was actually the "key." It unlocks the mystery of understanding the Bible and of knowing God's plan for the earth, given in the book of Revelation. The fulfillment of all things comes when great multitudes of believers know the Bible, recognize His voice, and obey His commands sent by His Spirit from heaven. Years back the Holy Spirit revealed that the word "vocation" meant "to have the incitement (urging) of God," but this morning He revealed how each chapter of the book of Ephesians shows a different aspect of our relationship with God through the Holy Spirit. Each point of view given in each chapter of Ephesians was revealing a fuller understanding of this necessary "key." To understand the book of Revelation, and the entire Bible, we must be led by His living Spirit. In this way we develop our faith to be like Jesus, who said He only did what He heard and saw the Father do.

Here are how the "keys" were used to emphasize His truth in the book of Ephesians:

- Chapter 1: We are children of God meant to have power over every name that is named (Ephesians 1:5, 19, 21).
- Chapter 2: We are the house of God, the resting place of His Spirit; we replace the tabernacle and the temple (on earth) (Ephesians 2:21–22).
- Chapter 3: We, the Jew and the Gentile, are made one by the sin sacrifice of Jesus Christ on the cross for all sin (Ephesians 3:6).
- Chapter 4: We are taught by Jesus, not by the devil, and what comes out of our mouths identifies who our source is (Ephesians 4:21–22).
- Chapter 5: We, the Bride of Christ, are to be filled with His Word and Spirit so that we think on Him, for a bride loves her Husband, her thoughts are on Him, she loves Him above all else (Ephesians 5:26). Hearing His living voice changes us.
- Chapter 6: The Word of God is our spiritual weapon. We must know it, practice it, speak it, young or old, rich or poor, employee or employer. For our battle is against spiritual darkness. Speak the sword of the Spirit of God! Act on it! Overcome (Ephesians 6:17). (His utterance, His speaking, His command.)

THE TRAP

In prayer today I was led to recite Psalm 91. As I got to the fourteenth verse, "because He has set His love upon me I will deliver him; I will set him on high because He hath known my name," the Lord revealed that "the great deception in My people is that they are in a trap, believing the lie that their first love is to do what others think, believe, or say is truth. Because they have not spent their time to engrave Me, My Word, upon their heart, they no longer recognize My voice and they ignore My direction; I am not first priority in their lives. They limit My ability to deliver them from the enemy because of their corrupted belief. The trap has been set and they are in it. Because of the blindness of their heart, because of ignorance of My Word, they don't realize the danger. Just as animals in the country go carelessly about their day looking for sustenance, so people without My supernatural guidance go carelessly about their day. In the case of the animal the alarm doesn't go off until the door slams shut on the trap and they can't get out. Now that animal is quite angry and when the trap setter comes the animal's attention is completely focused on his enemy. Unfortunately for the animal it is too late. To avoid the trap set by the enemy, the answer is for all humanity to focus on My Word, hear My voice, see My plan in their imagination, and follow it before the trap is sprung (Romans 8:24–25). 'I will deliver you,' says our God."

Creatures of Habit

That's the way I <u>always do it</u>.

I'm <u>use</u> to that way.

That's how <u>I was raised</u>.

It's a <u>Habit</u>.

That's their <u>routine</u>.

That's Our <u>Custom</u>.

I'm <u>familiar</u> with that.

They are <u>brainwashed</u>!

That was <u>ingrained</u> in me.

<u>Force</u> of Habit.

They're <u>very religious</u>!

He was <u>trained to</u> respond that way.

They are <u>stuck in a rut</u>!

It's a <u>conditioning</u> of the Heart.

That's our <u>tradition</u>!

She is <u>set in her ways</u>.

Humans are <u>creatures of Habit</u>.

CHAPTER 1

CREATURES OF HABIT

THE WISDOM OF GOD IS ABOVE
THE EDUCATION OF THE WORLD

THE FULFILLMENT OF ALL THINGS is God's wisdom given to every man. The original twelve disciples were not the highly educated religious leaders of the Jews. In fact, what they did know by religious understanding actually posed a great resistance to what Jesus was trying to teach them. They were regular, common men with a desire to know God. God's desire is for Jesus to instruct the ignorant, illuminating the truth so that they would know truth's source, the Most High. God never intended for men to be the source of knowledge of God for other men (Exodus 20:19–20). God's intention is for all men to know Him and to hear His voice and to obey (Jeremiah 31:33–34). Men more experienced and knowledgeable in the Word and Spirit are meant to be teachers and leaders to others. Their purpose should be to lead all men to the Word and the Spirit, the Living Christ, with the objective of all men being taught and guided by Jesus Christ Himself, the voice of God from heaven (Ephesians 4:17–21). God's desire is for every man to be able to know Him, to freely choose His way; free men, by their own free will, choosing to be His sons, to love Him (Exodus 20:1–21; John 1:12).

The advantage of the disciples who walked with Christ was that they knew Jesus Christ. They didn't have to read about Him to know Him; they lived with Him, they walked around with Him. For this reason they knew His character, so that when Jesus rose from the dead and gave them His Spirit to live in them, they knew His voice and could obey. The fulfillment of all things for us today is to know the Word of God, the Bible, so that we know Jesus, the Word (John 1:1, 14). Then we can accurately or justly recognize the living Spirit of God and obey (1 John 4:1; Romans 12:2). Just think of the multitudes of people all over the entire world being commanded by the voice of God from heaven through our intercessor, Jesus Christ (Romans 8:26–27). Our biggest hindrance to believing this is our own God-given nature of habitualness. Humans are habitual; we tend to do what we have always done. Also, we tend to do what the majority around us do. We don't like to change even if the change is good for us. A person tends to do what is bad for them, even when they believe a change would improve their life. Our nature is that strong. Since we were created with natures so dominantly ruled by habit and the influence of others, it seems evident that God made us this way for His good purpose. Considering this, we can conclude that we are intended by

God to habitually spend time with Him, with the final goal of being like Him.

So, here is the fulfillment, that we would read His Word, the Bible, know it, and obey it. Our great hindrance is that we don't believe we can know God. We think, by habit, that a priest or a preacher should confirm the truth of God. Then when they fail us we blame God and turn from trusting Him. Men, no matter what their position or their good nature, are susceptible to temptation and failure. That is why Jesus died for us; His atoning blood covers our inability to be perfect.

Finally, the commanding evidence in the Bible of the written Word's importance is that it is one of the three treasures kept in the Ark of the Covenant. Also, there is a warning given by God that the dragon, Satan, would hate those who keep the commandments of God (Revelation 12:17). "Keep" here means to guard from loss or injury, by keeping your eye upon. In other words, know God's word in order to be safe. History shows us that those in power have killed the educated priest and preacher for translating the Bible into the language that the common man could understand. This is proof that the world is against God's Word. Furthermore, the most abundant evidence of the powerful deception of our common enemy is that the Bible today in our nation is so freely available and yet, according to a George Barna survey and also what I have found, only about ten percent of Christians have read the Bible one time, cover to cover, let alone have continued reading it so they will know it.

So, the finality of this is that we are not at war with each other; we are at war with the invisible hidden presence of a demonic entity whose sole power is to deceive us. Our weapon is the Word of God administered by the power of God, being directed by the voice of God, the Holy Spirit.

The fulfillment of all things is for us to know God, obey God fearlessly till death do we part from this fleshly temple we call our body. "In whom ye also are builded together for an habitation of God through the Spirit" (Ephesians 2:22).

The education of the world comes after the knowledge of the Bible. This education is simply to be used as a vehicle to transport the good news of a God who loves and cares for us, but also requires us to restrain ourselves, seeking the peace of God, His residing presence in us superior to all other influences (Proverbs 9:10).

REBELLION AND RIGHTEOUSNESS HAVE A COMMON DENOMINATOR

The common denominator is the heart. The conditioning of the heart is paramount. How the heart is trained or conditioned bears the most weight on which spirit will be followed. The passion of the heart cannot be the judge of a person's goodness, because the conditioning of the heart, which way it has been trained, will determine that judgment. Either rebellion or right standing with God is determined by the words that come out of the mouth, not the passion of the heart. Jesus said, "Out of the abundance of the heart the mouth speaks" (Luke 6:45; Matthew 12:34). This is also how the evil religious false prophet, which comes in the last of the last days, is recognized, for he will look like a lamb, but speak like the devil (Revelation 13:11).

Passion is important to both the rebellious heart and the righteous heart. There is, however, a crucial difference. The critical power in rebellion is the impassioned heart, whereas the critical power of the righteous is the inspiration of the Holy Ghost, the insight to see His direction, and the incitation to know when to act. This direction of the Holy Ghost gives power to the righteous heart. This is the difference between religion and righteousness. The righteous will do what the discerned voice of the Holy Ghost says. That voice is perceived by a heart which has been conditioned through knowledge of the Bible and has been trained by God through remembering His character. The religious will tend to obey what they have been taught by mankind. They never go past natural instruction to the instruction of Jesus Christ through the same Spirit of God that directed Him (Ephesians 4:20–21), that is, the Holy Ghost that dwells in us. This is the difference between being cold or hot for the Lord (Revelation 3:15–16). In the Bible God says, "If you keep my word I will give you an open door," (Revelation 3:7–8), and also, "If I knock at your door, and you hear, and open the door, I will come in to you" (Revelation 3:20). So, again, the common denominator is the conditioning of the heart. Whether the person is either righteous or rebellious is keyed to either the passion of the human heart or the supernatural direction of the Holy Ghost. The Holy Ghost always agrees with the Bible and its principles, and gives direction to the heart which is filled with the knowledge of God. The power of the righteous is the ability to hear from the throne of God through the open door of the heart to the open door of heaven (Revelation 4:1; 22:14).

THE PRINCIPLE PROBLEM AND THE COMPREHENSIVE CURE

This knowledge was given as I lay awake on my bed at 7:07 in the morning on Sunday, the 13th of November, 2016. The strong, almost audible voice of my Lord caused me to jump up out of bed to write these words. This is what I heard:

Habitualness is broken by the voice of the Holy Ghost. God's direction is known by the testimony of the Holy Ghost agreeing with the written Word of God and/or His principle. The key of the book of Revelation, the Bible, and this walk with Christ, is that we must each, individually, overcome deception. Jesus has the keys of hell and death (Revelation 1:18) and the key of David (Revelation 3:7; Isaiah 55:2–4). The key of David was that he had the Holy Ghost guiding him. He, the Holy Ghost, was given to David as an example of what God is offering to all who would believe and have faith (James 2:23). He, the Holy Ghost, is a witness, a leader, and a commander to the people. The most challenging questions we face are, will we trust enough to spend the time to seek to know Him? Will we love Him, Jesus Christ, the Word, the Holy Ghost with all our heart? (That is, will our heart leap for knowledge of Jesus?) Will we love Him with all our mind (what we normally think and dream of), and will we love Jesus with all our soul (that is, our normal respiratory breathing)? In other words, will we seek to love Jesus Christ all the time with all our life? (John 14:23; Deuteronomy 6:5). Jesus taught this same thing in Matthew 22:37.

Here are three strong examples of powerful believers in the Bible who followed this fundamental learning process in order to fulfill the Father's will on earth. Jesus is one of these, and His example perhaps is enough for us to follow in His footsteps.

1. David was trained to know the Word of God by writing songs about God and then singing them as he was shepherding sheep in the wilderness. It is said that David wrote almost half of Psalms in the Bible. (First Samuel 16:16, 18 says that David was a cunning player of the harp.) When his schooling was completed, the Holy Ghost came on him to give him the fullness of God's power (1 Samuel 16:13).

2. Jesus was first trained in knowledge of the Word (Luke 2:42, 47). Then He was baptized with the Holy Ghost for the fullness of the power of God to work through Him (Matthew 3:13–17).

3. The disciples of Christ were first trained by Jesus Christ by walking with Him for three and a half years. Then they were baptized with the Holy Ghost for power to

do the work of the Father on earth (Acts 1:8, 2:4, 3:12). (The Holy Ghost is a witness, the power agreeing to your knowledge of the Bible.)

Each of these examples shows that the power of God, needed to finish His work on earth, is gained by the believers first training to know the true God, the written Word. Then afterwards, being <u>fully confident</u> in who God is, they are ready to discern His voice and accomplish God's desire for their life. This is for their safety and for fulfillment of life, perfect communication.

Our vocation is to be perfectly led by the Spirit of God (Ephesians 4:1; Romans 12:2). Our calling, our vocation, is to know and obey our Father in heaven. The battle in ourselves and in churches is the question, or possibly the doubt of unbelief asking us, "Can God really speak to me?" or "Will the Holy Ghost truly guide?" Maybe it's the thought, "Isn't our duty just to know the Word of God and do our best not to break the laws of God?" Or maybe we have the thought, "It's not our responsibility to be concerned with being instantly, minute by minute led by the voice of God."

Herein is revealed the root of the issue; people are creatures of habit and so what they believe, by conditioning or routine, becomes habit. Habit turns into a kind of truth that becomes very difficult to change, even when we want to. This is the motivation for recognizing the unction of the Holy Ghost (1 John 2:20); He is the only sure habit breaker. Our job is to know the Bible so that we can have confidence that we are hearing and following the correct Spirit (1 John

2:3, 4:1; Hebrews 4:11). Since the truth is verified by two or more witnesses that agree, we can prove the Living Voice of God, because it will line up with our knowledge of the written Word of God and lead us into all truth (Numbers 35:30).

So the deception that would keep us from knowing the truth is that our human nature is drawn to do what we love the most and what we think on the most. That's how we demonstrate our love (John 14:15, 21, 23). If we do not train ourselves to know the Bible and discern the voice of God, then corruption becomes our guide. This corrupt conditioning develops our resistance to the Holy Ghost's attempt to turn us back to Him, to His way. Then the deception is sealed as we become drawn to people or groups of people who love what we love. We become hardened in our corrupted way, even warring against the Spirit of Grace that attempts to bring us to the heart of our Father in heaven.

So the deadly weapon that the darkness of this world uses against us is our corrupted nature of habit. It turns our desire to dwell, or habitate, with God, to the desire for others of like corrupted minds. In them we find false comfort in two or more people who love and agree with us, becoming our false witnesses. In this dark ignorance our blackened heart becomes rampantly greedy for all uncleanness (Ephesians 4:17–19). At this juncture sin grows at an exponential rate and fellowship with the Light of Jesus Christ becomes very difficult (1 John 1:6; Romans 1:28).

THE THINGS THAT HINDER GOD AND HELP THE DEVIL AND HURT YOU

Doing the work that God has created for you to accomplish on earth has to do first with legality. We as believers in Jesus Christ know that the sin-free sacrifice of His life on the cross breaks the curse of our sins in our life when we believe in Him. But if by the confession of our mouth we give evidence that our heart doubts this truth we give place to the devil in our life. So the devil, or corrupted belief, has been given a certain amount of rulership in our lives (Ephesians 4:27).

We must guard our heart so that what comes out of our mouth is the truth of the Word of God and not the corruption of the devil's lies. So one of our most important jobs is to really listen to the words that come out of our mouth and identify any evidence that proves our hearts are not right with our legal proclamation that we are the children of God.

Another valid accusation of the enemy comes when we do what God directs us to and then for varied reasons we doubt that we accomplished His desires. When we seek God for direction in our life and realize what He is directing us to do, then our duty is to do that thing and not to get stuck trying to justify the results. Our job is to love God, work to know Him through His Word, then practice hearing His voice and obeying. So we know Him, hear His voice, then obey. Our job is to obey. Our job is not to understand or anticipate His plan. We simply hear the voice of our Boss and do what He said to do.

Of course, believing God is a good God and possessed of the greatest integrity, we know we can trust Him.

So, by being aware of the words we speak we can guard ourselves and gain trust that we are hearing God our Father in heaven. We can determine that we are not being deceived by our own corrupt understanding or possibly by dark persuasions. Here are four words for feelings we may sense in ourselves. When we are aware of these feelings we should speak out the Word of truth from knowledge of the Bible, which will draw us near to God and cause the corruption to flee (James 4:7–8).

1. Jealousy (Envy): Spiteful malice and resentment over another's advantage. (related words: grudging, resentment, covet, crave, long, want, yearn.)

2. Pridefulness (Lack of humility): We should lack all signs of pride, be humble, show appreciation, be modest, unassuming, unpretentious. The opposite is to be overbearing, proud, conceited, arrogant, vain, showy. Humility is not trying to do right, it's knowing Him! Humility comes from knowing God, causing us to realize He is our protector, provider. He gives us strength, intelligence, favor, life! Our obedience to Him destroys the pride in ourselves.

3. Hatred: Some related words are: abomination, animosity, antipathy, hostility, ill will, disgust, scorn, abhor, detest, loathe, despise, disdain, resent, to feel extreme enmity or dislike. (An acceptable hatred is to hate evil and to love righteousness.)

4. Reject (Rejection): Decline. Related words are: eliminate, exclude, shut out, discard, deny (ourselves and others).

God desires us to know Him so we might obey Him. His desire for us is obedience, not sacrifice (Hosea 6:3, 6 ; Isaiah 1:11; 2 Corinthians 10:4–6).

MUSIC DEVELOPS STRONG HABITS

It seems that music gives the easiest access to the mind and heart of a person. Setting words to music is the easiest and fastest way to remember and engrave words into a heart. When music is used to memorize it gives two ways to access the material, by recognizing the tune, or a word or phrase in the song. A problem with music is that the style of music and the words together must be the two witnesses that agree to truth. The message must come through both with strength and clarity. If change is to be attempted, you are fighting a person's engraved heart, which is very difficult (Zechariah 3:9; Psalm 119:11).

Music can also be used to unify groups of people. A national anthem will unify a nation. A love song sung in a certain language will touch that language group. However, music's potential to bring people together also causes great hostility between generations that have been conditioned to prefer different music styles. Our human nature causes us to fight any change from our favored form or style of music, and this causes great contention between generations. This is especially controversial in churches, where music is used in singing about God and as a vehicle to lead congregations into worship.

Music is a wonderful way to memorize Scripture, but I have only used this style of memorization on a very limited basis. Because I don't play an instrument or have a musical background I have only used this style of memorization when I was given a tape of Scripture verses set to music by my boss in 1995. I found that I would sing these Scripture verses and my day would become full of peace.

The style of memorization I use is word recognition and repetition. I find this allows the Lord to lead me by the Scripture He brings to my mind. The understanding brought by the memorization many times will lead me to the next area of revelation the Lord desires me to see. So this is a simple way for me to stay on His path and be led by His direction as the next thought or Scripture comes to mind. This way of receiving direction builds a deeper, closer relationship with our Father in heaven as He leads a person to greater trust in Him. As inner peace grows, so does trust and confidence in Him, allowing a believer to become a more willing servant, even a friend. For as we hear Him speak, we begin to see His plan for our life. Our corrupted imaginations are replaced by His divine fulfillment for the nations. Perfect Peace (John 14:27).

THE AMAZING THING ABOUT THE PROCESS

God wants us to know that He directs our life. He wants us to trust Him, to have faith in Him that He really does have our best interests at heart. One of the ways He does this is by giving us heart-certainty in the way He leads us when our mind doesn't see the complete picture. One of the underlying principles that the Lord develops in us is obedience to His voice in our heart, not our logical mind. This is where the Scripture in Ephesians 3:19 applies, that the fullness of Jesus Christ comes as we fill ourselves with the knowledge of the Word. Then we can go past the contents of our limited minds to the fullness of the revealed voice of God from heaven, by recognizing His voice as it agrees with the known Word.

So, for me, the amazing thing about the process of memorization was how the Lord used it to take me to the end of myself, and then allowed me to see the new direction He was leading. I experienced a good example of God breaking limits when I came to NFCC (Northern Florida Christian Center). I knew God called me to work there and accepting His call took a leap of faith, because the maintenance job would severely reduce our income. So the Lord overcame one limitation in my life, the concern about our income, but now after six years I believed my purpose at NFCC was complete. I had done all I could do to build a systematic way of managing the two hundred and forty acres and I felt that it was time for me to leave and pursue making more money. As I began to plan my departure from my job, everyone I counseled with told me not to do it. Finally, I heard the direction of the Lord, "Wait, I have something else for you."

Now I knew in my heart that God's direction was to wait. I was excited about this, but I had no idea how long I would wait, or what I was waiting for. Three months later at a Saturday men's Christian breakfast, the speaker told us that you must know God's Word in order to stand fast in obedience to God and to overcome the attacks of the realms of darkness. Right away I knew this was the Lord giving me the answer to what I was waiting for. What I didn't know was if I could memorize, how long would it take, and how much I should memorize. I had no idea how the memorization would greatly influence my confidence and trust in my ability to hear God's voice giving direction to my life. What I found out far surpassed the limits of what I could understand in my natural capabilities! I found that the Lord opened a door to heaven to hear His voice for me with more clarity and certainty than ever before!

What is most striking about this process of memorization in my life is how I was motivated at first purely by amazement that I could actually remember Scripture; I didn't know it was possible. Then I was also excited about the thought that it would help me become steady, stable in my Christian walk. Up to that time I had been very much up and down with my faith and trust that God would actually provide. I was always looking for some miraculous move or act or word or dream from God to know what to do next. That made living this Christian life a very precarious thing; it was nerve-wracking.

Now, I first realized a surprising thing as I began by memorizing popular partial Scripture verses. I discovered it as I went on to learn the whole Scripture, and especially as I learned the whole chapter that contained the Scripture. Then I realized that what I thought the Scripture meant before memorizing was quite different than what I was taught by God, by Christ, the Holy Spirit as I actually began to know the verse. This was very liberating. I gained peace and confidence and stability I never knew in Scripture and in God. There was almost no outside approval, but mainly confusion and some outright hostility from Christians. So after about a year of thoroughly enjoying memorizing and learning I was very surprised when into my mind came the thought, "Memorize the book of Revelation and I'll show you the key." I impulsively laughed, then just as quickly I said, "What the heck, if You say so, then it can be done." So even now the amazement continues, for just last month, October 2018, the Lord whispered to my mind and heart, "The vocation and the key are one. Now you know the purpose of the book of Revelation, that you know My written Word so that you can hear, discern, and obey the voice of My Spirit and do My work on earth as My only begotten Son did. You realize that since I have become your leadership I can never be taken from you, as long as I lead you by My Spirit from heaven. Your vocation is to be inspired by discerning My voice, to have the key to hear My command from the open door of the throne room of heaven. This is what successful last days living will be about. This is how My saints will overcome" (Revelation 3:20).

Also, after I finished the book of Revelation (1/30/04) I would spend the next four months reviewing all the memorized Scripture, reading through the book of Revelation by memorization recital two more times. Through this inundation of pure uncorrupted Scripture flowing through my mind and heart I was receiving almost constant communication from God, giving me completely new understanding. Again there was nobody who could confirm or deny the validity of the understanding because nobody else had heard such things. It was painful but at the same time I realized that this is how so many new denominations start. First there comes to you the glorious revelation and understanding. Then you become upset because no authority, no person validates you except the Spirit of God and His Word. Then yet another sect splits off from a group. So I continued to memorize new Scripture as the Lord would lead me. After four months of reviewing the former Scriptures, on June 9, 2004, I started on a new Scripture, Romans chapter eight. At this time I knew my quiet, peaceful job as a maintenance man at my beloved Northern Florida Christian Center was coming to an end.

HOW MEMORIZATION IS HINDERED

Our entire calling is to know the voice of God so that we can recognize the Holy Spirit speaking to us, and that we can identify the devil's lies and act on God's voice.

In my life, the Lord has used memorization as the most effective method to help me toward this calling. People resist accepting this method because they have been wrongly conditioned. They assume that you memorize so you can know more Scripture verses than other people, for the purpose of demonstrating your knowledge to others. That's not the purpose of memorization. In fact, I have experienced that to use memorization for the purpose of showing someone else your knowledge actually hinders God's ability to allow you to know Him. You see, what you prove something by, you become subject to (Romans 8:7). So, if the knowledge of the Word is proved by a person, we become subject to that person. However, through memorization God desires to develop our confidence in hearing His living voice so that we can be directed instantly by Him (Romans 12:2). So the true purpose of memorization is to train ourselves to know God's Word so that we can hear the Holy Spirit speak through Scripture. Then as He teaches us we become more confident in Him directing our life, allowing us to be a tool more ready for use by the Master's hand.

By the confidence builder of recognizing the voice of God, we cast away our unbelief (Hebrews 3:19). For the flesh that our spirit dwells in is enmity against God: for it is not subject to God, neither indeed can be (Romans 8:7). So we learn to know the voice of God when He teaches us new things by His expounding (Ephesians 4:21) the Scriptures that we have labored to know (Hebrews 4:11–12). This effort that we are commanded to make allows us to love God and allows Him to direct His love through us. ("If you love Me, keep My commandments." [John 14:15, 21,23, 24].) This is true love, to know the Father, by knowing the Son, the Word (John 1:1, 14).

THE WAY TO KNOW GOD

The purpose of detailing the memorization process that I use is to give anyone interested an example of the steps over which the Lord led me. Through these steps others can also be guided by the voice of God in their specific path. The purpose of life in Christ is to know very well the particular role you fill in His objective. So the voice of God may direct you to an area of the Bible that someone else doesn't need to know with perfection, but which you do. The understanding, or revelation, which comes from memorization is a great confidence builder, causing our trust in God to grow. Gaining this understanding is the foundational motivation for the effort memorizing requires.

The key concept I hope readers will grasp is the length of time it took for the Lord to teach me that my responsibility was to know Him and hear His voice and obey. My obligation was not to get other people to agree with me or for me to fall in line to what they said was right. It took years, really decades, for me to fully realize that my duty is to God first! I had to realize that I must love everything else less than I love Him. Otherwise, whatever takes His place in my priorities will control me. Possibly you sense the same hindrance in your life?

21

My original period of memorization started on May 27, 2002, and ended on June 21, 2004, after two years of endeavor. I considered reviewing in this book each case of the Scriptures I was led to memorize, but it became obvious that this would be far too lengthy and perhaps unproductive. For this reason, I decided not to list my original memorized Scripture verses.

However, what I believe will be helpful is an account of the way the Spirit of God led me to the first verses that started my introduction to knowing Him fully. First, I acknowledged that a feeling that dominated my thoughts was against what I knew the Bible said. So, I found verses that spoke to this truth of God and engraved them upon my heart. Next, when Scripture kept coming to mind I recognized that God was trying to get me to think more about that Word, so I did. The third motivation the Lord used for me to memorize was occasions when I was rebuked by a person or by God's Spirit in an area in which I was weak. He used these occasions to teach me what I couldn't see. The fourth reason I would memorize a verse was to answer a question I had about something in the Bible. The next reason I memorized was that I knew from the Bible that I should be experiencing certain emotions, and I wanted those experiences. The sixth reason was simply to respond to a note I had written in my Bible, to know a verse better.

The next to last reason I memorized was a desire to know the whole thought that surrounded a Scripture verse. This meant I would engrave on my heart the Scriptures around the verse, or the entire chapter or book the verse was in. Lastly, and what I believe summarizes all the eight reasons to memorize, I memorize in response to the Lord's leading. That is the simplicity of the purpose of memorizing Scripture, to know the living voice of God, that we might obey Him.

These words testify and direct attention to a further truth. I experienced rejection in Christian circles at that time. The witness of the Holy Spirit to the written Word and to my spirit was not sufficient evidence to overturn most people's belief. I had very limited positive response when I shared what I had been taught (Ephesians 4:21). Because I had so much trust in and knowledge of the integrity of my Christian associates I was brought to an impasse. If I pushed what I knew was truth it would cause great divisions and break the unity of peace. Also, at the same time I was greatly curious as to why people would not even want to discuss what I had seen, and why just the thought of differences would evoke such anger. The Scripture "all things work toward good" (Romans 8:28) and "here is the patience of the saints" (Revelation 14:12) kept coming to mind, so I waited. I waited ten years, from 2005 to 2015. Then I began to memorize new Scriptures that the Lord brought to mind. During this time the Lord also brought about understanding of the strong resistance to the voice of His Spirit, even in myself and among Christians. The Holy Spirit also exhibited to me my lack of integrity with Him, which greatly surprised me. So all in all

God's wisdom in telling me to wait become very apparent, and I was thankful to Him.

So, at this time, if God reveals this to be truth to you, use it as a springboard to begin laboring (Hebrews 4:11) to know Him better by knowing His Bible, the written Word of God spoken to our forefathers. If I have understood correctly how evil gains power and what God's purpose is in His fulfillment of all things, the church as we know it will be controlled by evil leaders in the last of the last days. At that time we will need to have confidence in hearing, knowing, and acting on God's voice speaking to us. We will need to be as Jesus was, led by the voice of His Father, as it is written in Matthew 4:4, 7, and 10. Act as Christ acted, moved only by His Father's direction as it is spoken and aligns with the written Word and/or principle.

CHAPTER 2

HISTORY

CIRCLE LOGIC

SOMETIMES THE LORD WILL BRING clarity in His instruction by putting mental pictures to His voice. This morning the Lord taught me three things in a dream. He taught me that, first, His desire is for me to hear and obey for my life direction. Second, the resistance, which is the power of our flesh, hinders His fulfillment in my life, and third, the obstacle, which is corrupt habit, must be overcome. Simply put, what I just stated covers three basic points. They are:

1. God's desire is for me to hear His command, His voice from heaven, and as a proper servant to understand and obey. He says, "Obey Me."

2. The Lord gave further instruction that the resistance that hinders is the natural desire of my flesh. As the flesh realizes that it has my attention, it begins to direct me away from desiring God to desiring fulfillment in

the flesh. Ultimately the path leads to lack of life, lack of my spirit's inspiration, and finally to spiritual death.

3. The obstacle that must be overcome is the corrupt conditioning of the soul (mind, will, emotions), that is, the way you receive instructions. If you always check with God before you act then you insure that you are truly following His instruction and that His instruction has not changed. The obstacle that must always be overcome is habit, natural habit. Check the supernatural Guide, the agreement of the written Word of God with His living Spirit, to confirm that His instructions have not changed.

Here is the dream, the mental picture:

I was at the Northern Florida Christian Center in what must have been the dining room. My old friend Tom and I were sitting in chairs facing each other. Tom was giving light rebuke, trying to give me gentle yet firm correction. I was frustrated at my inability to understand Tom or my lack of proper expression so that he could see his error.

At this point something came over me and I leaned forward and said with a strong voice, "You see, Tom, here is the problem. You have been conditioned to obey leadership on earth regardless of whether that leadership is hearing from heaven or not. Because of this conditioning, your flesh insists that you conform to error from the instituted chain of command. Now you are resisting course corrections by the Holy Spirit because what He says doesn't fit into your ingrained protocol."

I continued to speak, "Tom, the proper chain of command is for us to hear God from heaven and obey. We can follow chain of command leadership on earth, as long as the Lord approves. If, however, we sense error compared to what we perceive is Holy Ghost instruction, we must verify this instruction by the confirmation in the Word and by agreement of our spirit with the Holy Spirit, then act on His living direction. Our reverence has to be to His voice above all (Psalm 34:7). We may sense that fear has a sway on our life and that the fear is of natural consequences. When that happens, we should, no, we must, prove our course by earnestly seeking the Lord to know that our direction is of His leading. There must be reverence to His authority, and certainty that we are not responding to the fearful intonation of this body of flesh which is our temporary habitation (Hebrews 5:7–8; Luke 22:42–44)."

At this moment of passionate inspiration of the Holy Ghost speaking through me, I became aware of what seemed to be many people. They were out of my direct vision and behind Tom, and they were looking at us. I took my gaze off Tom and looked to confirm what I sensed with my peripheral vision. As I changed my focus from Tom to the distraction of my natural vision, I saw many faces and all of them were spellbound, staring with amazement at me, enthralled by the words flowing out of my mouth. Immediately I dropped my gaze from the people and became aware of a swelling throughout my body and my soul. I no longer had any words to say to Tom. I knew, somehow, that I was lost and I didn't know why or what had happened.

At this point in the dream I was outside myself looking at the scene. Tom and I were still facing each other, but now my head was hung low, looking at the ground. Again, as I stated, I knew I was lost, without any Holy Ghost direction and not knowing why or what I should do. I was feeling very powerless and worthless.

At this moment the Holy Ghost, that is the Spirit of God which was in Jesus Christ when He walked on earth in His body of flesh, this Spirit began to speak and instruct, teaching me what I did not understand (Ephesians 4:20–21).

The Lord instructed me, "Pat, when you took your attention off Me, you were no longer in the spirit (Revelation 1:10). You allowed your natural eyes and senses to distract you from focusing on what I was speaking; you shut the door of heaven. You need to fully realize the danger of your fleshly body. It has great power over the direction it wants you to go. In fact, as you experienced when your attention went to the people, your flesh unconsciously swelled with pride, causing the doorway of heaven to close (Revelation 3:7–8). You were then left without the Leader and Commander of your soul (Isaiah 55:3–4) to direct your way. In fact, the only way you can effectively and consistently overcome the natural corruption of your flesh is for Me to put a guard around your spirit (Psalm 34:7). When you reverence Me there is an angel stationed to protect you. I am your only sure defense, but you shut the doorway to heaven and open a hole in your wall of protection when you allow distractions to keep you from following My way. Your body is a small room holding your spirit and corruption. That corruption lusts to steal, kill, and destroy all that you have. Your only defense against the darkness is to have your attention on Me."

At this time I was made aware of how this dream and the instruction given to me was information to be used as the complete outline for the third book, *All Things Are Fulfilled*. I realized that the premise of the book was quite simple, but the details of the premise could get very lengthy and complex. I knew the book was intended for those who already had faith in God, faith that the sacrificial, sin-free blood of His Son, Jesus Christ, covers our inadequacies, our sin. Also, the book is intended for those who have not yet come to the faith, but eventually will do so.

One of the most important points for the believer to understand is that the flesh, the corrupted flesh, is also ignorant and in enmity (Romans 8:7) against the Word of God and against faith in His voice. When corruption reaches a certain point, the heart becomes darkened and hardened, blind to the living things of God. At this point the flesh, the body, lusts to do evil and becomes greedy for it (Ephesians 4:17–19). This is the phenomenon we have been experiencing in American politics, and in today's media (November 2016 to today, November 2018).

You may ask the question, "How does circle logic give a complete outline of this book, *All Things Are Fulfilled*?" The key is faith. For it really seems the battle being waged today is for which faith people will believe is true. Basically, the two faiths are faith in God, or faith in man.

There is deception in both camps of thought. The people of the world believe they are logical, not faith-based. The Christians think they are faith-based but then are led by their denominational leaders above what God's voice would teach them.

The circle logic is that both camps of faith require you to believe, to trust and hope in the faith that you adhere to. So the "circle of the logic" isn't really the problem of deciding which way is true. The actual question that needs to be answered is which faith do you wish to live under? My desire is to live under the faith that gives me peace, but each person must make that determination by their own free will. The correct answer for me is faith in God, specifically the God of Jesus Christ, because who He is, and what He is about is written in the book called the Bible, and it states that He doesn't change (Hebrews 13:8). This faith, which could be described as knowledge of the Word combined with experience of obeying the recognized voice of God—this is faith with confidence in God. All we are required to do is believe He is true and to seek cognizance of Him by knowing His Word so that we can recognize His Spirit and be led in His way. You see, the Spirit of God does not waver from the written Word of God, so the two are one with God; they must agree in order to be the truth. Herein is stability which gives security, soundness, and peace (1 John 4:1).

Faith in man follows a set of laws that can be rewritten any time man decides to change the law. This is unstable, insecure, and difficult to manage, and is also contentious. This leads to war.

So, to be concise, the fulfillment of God is the good news that the kingdom of God shall be preached in all the world, giving witness to all nations that the kingdom of God is within you by God's Spirit dwelling within believers. By this Spirit you have access to God's direction for your life through the knowledge of Jesus Christ (Luke 17:21; John 14:23). This fulfillment was achieved by the faithful actions of our forefathers in the Bible.

First we see belief in God demonstrated by the faithful actions of Abraham and others. Then comes the law, given by Moses, which passed down God's direction for life as recorded in the Old Testament. Then, Jesus Christ, the sin-free Son of God came and sacrificed His perfect blood for the sins of the world. That sin was brought into our bodies by Adam's disobedience to God's command. When Adam ate of the tree of the knowledge of good and evil, he limited communication with God (Genesis 2:17, 3:11). Communication is reestablished through the Spirit of God which dwelt in Jesus Christ and is given to those who believe and have asked God's Spirit to rule their lives. In order to ensure that the Spirit a believer hears is Jesus Christ, they must know Him who is the breath of God, His living Word written in the Bible.

So, the fulfillment of all things is the spreading of the good news of Jesus Christ and the written Word of God to every nation on the earth, so that every person in every nation now has the choice, according to the authority of their nation's leadership, to have access to true leadership, the commandment of God from heaven through the spirit of Jesus (John 14:26).

THESE TWO POINTS MUST AGREE

There are two pinnacles, two points, two witnesses confirming truth that allow a believer to walk in the way of Jesus Christ with full trust and confidence in Him.

The Word of God is one of the two pinnacles. Faith in the voice of God is one of two pinnacles. By keeping these two points lining up continuously in a life, the direction of God from heaven is known and His path is followed.

History shows that men of faith are established by one or the other of these two pinnacles, and at times by both. Great acts are done by these men and they become prosperous, producing great wealth, large successful families, powerful kingdoms, and eventually powerful nations. With this power comes a temptation to stray from the path of the two pinnacles, faith and the written Word, and instead to do what human reasoning thinks will give them what they crave, which is the desire that is right in their own eyes (Judges 17:6, 21:25). The focus of life becomes the desire for the things in this world rather than the things that the two pinnacles, faith and the written Word, lead to along the path of life.

So, through the course of history nations come to a point of war, whether internal or external, resulting in scattering the power gained by one of the two pinnacles, or both. This leads not to what will happen by man's natural reasoning, but in the end to spreading the power of God by faith in Him, resulting in God's completion, His end or fulfillment (Daniel 12:7, to scatter the Holy Power).

The end result in His fulfillment is mature men who will follow the direction of God no matter what the tempting distractions are. These men are produced to rule and reign with God and Christ for eternity (Revelation 20:4).

As nations are formed in the image of God they are constantly being challenged by the desires of the natural man, not completely transformed by the Word and Spirit of God. This battle of resistance is a struggle that will either strengthen or weaken trust in God. It will force a choice between trust in God or trust in man's ability. In this environment natural man becomes stronger, continually threatening the desire for God in the people and the nation, causing the scattering of the holy power, the believers. This action of the evil strong man causes the man of God to grow stronger in God and fight for righteousness, or give up and give in to the darkness.

The key to winning the battle and overcoming the dark persuasion is to understand our strength in the power of God as humankind and how ignorance of this strength ends in our overthrow. You see, we must first fight in the supernatural realm to win in the natural realm. Ignorance of the knowledge of God causes confusion, first on an individual level, then in the family and eventually the nation, causing the destruction of that which faithful men built. This dependence on the strength of mankind is our habitual nature. So we will do that which becomes a habit to us. We need the written Word of God firmly impressed, or engraved, upon our heart. It will guide us to all truth and righteousness, and the Spirit of God which agrees with His Word will also lead us along His path (John 16:13). Without these two pinnacles working in our life we will be overcome by the ever-strengthening power of men grouped together in the strength of men, void of the Holy Spirit's direction, nor confirmed by knowledge of the Bible.

Having only one of the two pinnacles is not everlasting. Either one by itself ends in powerful men or groups of men controlling the people. God's desire is for our desire to be toward Him. The problem is that for our desire to be toward God we must have confidence in Him. It requires us to trust that He loves us. To acquire this level of assurance requires us to know Him and to think on Him, to love Him. When we love someone or something, the thing we love fills our hearts and minds, and from the fullness of our hearts and minds our mouths speak continually (Luke 6:45; Psalm 139:23–24; Proverbs 4:23, 28:26; Jeremiah 17:9). So this goes back to the key of the two pinnacles, the Word of God and confidence in the voice of God. You see, these are really one. For the written Word of God is the spoken Word of God written down by faith that it was God who spoke it. Also, the faith of God is to believe that you can hear the voice of God. The power of God comes in the individual when that person can identify by faith the Spirit that is speaking to them (1 John 4:1). Then, by discerning it is God speaking, obeying with full confidence, and acting on God's direction by being <u>one in Him,</u> fulfillment is achieved (Deuteronomy 6:4–6).

SPIRITUAL UNREST IS A SIGNPOST OF THE COMING TRUTH

The six sects of Jews at Jesus' time are a shadow of the multitude of Christian sects at this time. Let us learn and be prepared.

At the time Jesus walked the earth, none of the six Jewish sects (the Scribes, Pharisees, Sadducees, Essenes, Zealots, and Nazarites), as a group accepted Him as the Messiah. Similarly, at the present time on earth there are a multitude of large Christian sects, or churches, that cannot agree what it will be like when Jesus returns.

If we use the model of the Old Testament to get an idea of what it will be like at the end of the New Testament, we see that organized religion didn't quite understand what was happening when Jesus came among His brothers, the Jews. Only those individuals who recognized Jesus for who He was gave Him honor and obedience. It seems very likely to parallel what will happen in our time. It will be individuals who will recognize the times, know Jesus, the recorded Word, the Bible, and be practiced at hearing His living voice, the Holy Spirit, and obeying. Having full trust and confidence in Him, this is the faith needed to overcome the fear that will dominate the earth.

SYNOPSIS OF THE MATURING CHURCH

Here is a concise snapshot of the people or times or church that defines the maturing process through the course of the Bible and the church age, to this very day.

Normal religion, or what we call church, has always been maturing, and changing. The process is natural, but because of human nature we resist change (humans are creatures of habit). The point here is that to resist change is to resist God. If God had intended for us to never change, our spiritual forefathers would have remained the same.

It seems that God's plan for the earth and its people was simply to create a people that God could fellowship or hang out with. Not a people forced by a law to either obey or be condemned, but a people like Him that freely want to do the right thing. He desires a people that love Him and whom He can love, just as we love to be with family that love us and want the best for each other. So God is producing in us on earth, for His eternal purpose, a forever family in heaven (1 John 1:3).

It seems there has to be evil in order for people to have a choice. Evil is defined as disobedience to God. Revealing the outcome of evil is a slow process. Evil only cares for that which it can see and imagine in its <u>own</u> concept. Evil takes control and forces people to conform to its desires or it punishes quickly. Evil moves fast, using fear and violence. God moves slowly, allowing mercy and grace to change the human heart to His heart. He brings about the realization that growth in eternal life is worth sacrificing the things that can be gotten on this physical earth (Psalm 19:10).

The point is that it takes much time to produce in mankind what God desires. The suffering that is endured is an essential part of the process (Hebrews 5:8).

For us on earth today, the evidence that God is bringing His process to completion can be seen in one important indicator: there is no continent in this earth to which the truth of God's Word has not come. Also, there is no place for believers in the Bible and the Spirit of God to run in order to escape the dangers coming, except to know and trust God more than ever before.

This is God's purpose, to spread His love to all the people in the earth, His chosen ones, both the Jew and the Gentile. Each person has the opportunity to choose His way on their own (Matthew 28:19).

He also is maturing His disciples to rule with Him during the 1,000 year reign of God and Christ (Revelation 20:4).

So change in the way we serve and worship God is ever maturing, and that means changing. Changing, although it means differing from what is normal, is still conforming to His Word, His Spirit, and His way or principle.

"The Lord is merciful and gracious, slow to anger and plenteous in mercy" (Psalm 103:8).

THEY STARTED THE WORK WE ARE FINISHING

God's desire is to fellowship, to be with those like Himself. You see, if we never lost our perfect communication with God, we would never know how bad evil is. God does not want us ignorant to evil's existence, but to resist evil and to imagine and desire only good (Genesis 3:22–24). So, there is a good purpose for all things. God's desire is to fellowship with those whose willing desire is to be with Him. There is a difference between having fellowship with a person who is forced to obey and being with someone who loves to be around you. We are being proved by God in this container, this vessel of our body on earth. This is the crucible called earth, and our battle to obey God comes from resistance, both outside and within ourselves. The battle that God designed is to accomplish an expected end. He wants us to enjoy Him as much as He desires to enjoy us. This time capsule of earth is bringing about, step by step, century by century, generation by generation, a fuller understanding of God's purpose.

The first step was the beauty of creation and the time of Adam and Eve in the garden with God (Genesis 2:1–25). Next came the eating of the forbidden, evil fruit, which caused them to be afraid of their Father, God. Adam and Eve believed the deception of evil and hid from fellowship with God (Genesis 3:8, 11). Not wanting to be near God, but obeying the voice of peer pressure, the advice of the serpent and Eve, Adam joined in disobedience, instead of fully trusting in God, possibly with the hope of saving Eve from death by joining himself with her, knowing His Father's love would intervene and pardon their sin (Genesis 3:13, 17). Afterward, communication with God was mixed with thoughts of evil, and evil began to grow. After several generations, from Adam to Noah, God saw that the wickedness of man was great in the earth and that every imagination of the thoughts of his heart was only evil continually (Genesis 6:5).

After that time, Noah found grace in the eyes of the Lord. Noah and his family of eight were saved in an ark, but all the rest of humanity were destroyed in the flood that covered the earth. Noah's example for us is that he believed the voice of God, diligently sought Him, and obeyed His voice, because of his reverence of God, by faith. Without written guidelines Noah minded the command of God (Hebrews 11:7; Genesis 6:13–14).

Afterwards Noah was given a sign from God of the bow in the cloud over the earth. Noah was told that this sign would be a token of God's covenant for all generations (Genesis 9:9–17).

At this step of the fulfilling of all things there was no Bible written. Noah was the only one who was just, and walking with God. These must have been very tough times to know God, recognize His voice, and obey, since only Noah was granted grace and called perfect, because he walked with God (Genesis 6:8–9).

During the generations from the end of the flood to the beginning of the building of the tower of Babel, the people didn't want to be scattered upon the face of the earth (Genesis 11:4). Their desire ran opposite to what God wanted them to do (Genesis 11:6–8; Daniel 12:6–7). So God confused them with different languages so they couldn't do whatever they imagined. It seems that without the restraining guidelines of God's influence, people will be drawn away from righteousness toward wickedness, which suggests that there is a basic flaw in humanity. Without the suppressing influence of the law of God and the forgiving grace of God we are destined to be overwhelmed by the growing influence of darkness, becoming brainwashed by evil (Ephesians 4:18–19).

Remember, according to the Bible, God created all things, and He has given all people the ability to hear His voice. King David spoke in Psalm 19:3, "There is no speech nor language, where their voice is not heard." He has a plan for all that we see happening. Our advantage today in America is that we still have the freedom to look back on church history, look back at our own national origin, see where we have fallen off course, and make the necessary corrections.

One great asset we have in this place and time is the amount of reference material available at our fingertips for gaining knowledge of the Bible. Never in any generation has the common man had this kind of accessibility to know Christian/Church history and learn from it, to know God themselves, and to be free to seek Him with all their heart and to know that they know Him. Let's return to the next step in the generations that gives evidence of God's desire for each individual to be able to discern His plan and will for their life and have fellowship with Him.

After the people were scattered from each other unto all the earth, the man Abram comes on the scene (Genesis 11:26; Hebrews 11:8–10). Abram is the man who has faith to follow God. He is also the father of three religions: the father of the Jews, the Christians, and the Muslims. His name was changed to Abraham (Genesis 17:5), meaning "father of many" and at that time he was supernaturally able to conceive a son when he was ninety-nine years old (Genesis 17:17–19). His wife Sarah was ninety when she gave birth. Abram was seventy-five years old when he left his home in Ur (Genesis 11:26–28, 12:4), which is a little over one hundred miles northwest of present-day Kuwait. He traveled about 750 miles north and northwest to the land of Canaan in the area of the Dead Sea where Jerusalem is located (Genesis 11:31). He was looking for a city whose builder and maker was God (Hebrews 11:10).

Man's form of religion has never satisfied completely. If man's religions did, there would be only one way, but each of these religions have more than one division among themselves. It seems an interesting note that Abram believed he was told by God to leave his country, kindred, and his father's house without any written direction to follow (Genesis 12:1). So Abram would be without that which was most familiar to him, perhaps that which he relied on most, from which he derived his strength. That's just what these last days are driving us to do, which is ask ourselves, "Do we trust God or trust men?" It seems and is also written that when we are weak in our natural abilities, if we believe, have faith, in God, then our trust in God is strengthened (2 Corinthians 12:9). Again, God's desire is to scatter the power of the holy people (Daniel 12:7), doubtlessly so that we become stronger in Him. Also, as we are scattered we demonstrate this example of Holy, God-honoring living to new people who now have the opportunity to hear, believe, know, and obey.

The point is that our Father in heaven wants us to know Him by knowing His written Word, the Bible. It is an invitation from heaven, to us, inviting us to come to Him. He is giving us the free choice, in the United States of America, to choose Him or not. We also have the opportunity to be an example to the rest of the world which does not have access to the written Word of God. We can influence the world for good, and to know God. Moses instructed the people just before his passing to heaven,

> If thou shalt hearken unto the voice of the Lord thy God, to keep His commandments and His statutes which are written in this book of the law, and if thou turn unto the Lord thy God with all thine heart, and with all thy soul. For this commandment which I command thee this day, it is not hidden from thee, neither is it far off. It is not in heaven, that thou shouldest say, Who shall go up for us to heaven, and bring it unto us, that we may hear it, and do it? Neither is it beyond the sea, that thou shouldest say, Who shall go over the sea for us, and bring it unto us, that we may

hear it, and do it? But the word is very nigh unto thee, in thy mouth, and in thy heart, that thou mayest do it. (Deuteronomy 30:10–14)

The previous brief sketch illustrates a major theme, which is of faith building in the Bible, along with confidence and growing trust in hearing God's living voice. The purpose of the account is to bring awareness of the importance of God bringing the written Word to the common man. You see, to condense this time in the Bible from Abraham's appearance to the birth of the Jewish religion from Abraham's loins, it is essential to understand the great importance of the spoken Word of God being transferred into written form. The written Word of God has the highest seat of honor in the Jewish religion, and of course Christianity comes directly from the written Word; that is the authority. Jesus even said that these things must come about that the Scripture might be fulfilled (Matthew 5:17–18). So understand that to honor the written Word of God by knowing it is essential to having the fullness of life in Jesus Christ that He promised to us who would believe in Him. Otherwise, we are dependent on men, on pastors, priests, or rabbis leading us to truth, which is the process of God's desire, but not the fullness.

Jesus warns us not to be deceived by men (Matthew 24:4; Mark 13:5; Luke 21:8) and confirmed to the disciples that God is to be their director on earth (John 17:8, 11, 14–15, 17, 20–21). In other words, Jesus said this is what is going to happen and then this is how we get through it. So this compact summary of the Old Testament boils down to this truth: the spoken Word of God was transcribed in written form to announce the fulfillment of all things, the coming of the Savior of the world, to all mankind.

The three religions that came out of the loins of Father Abraham are, starting from the first: Judaism (started about 1812 B.C.), then Christianity (started about A.D. 33), and the Muslim religion (started about A.D. 610). Each of these has its own limitations.

First, Judaism places knowledge of the written Word of God, which is called Tanakh, at the highest honor. This is also the text used for the Christian faith, which Christians refer to as the Old Testament. The priests or rabbis instruct the people, so the common Jew's faith is limited by what is authorized by the heads of the religion, the rabbis. Also, conversion rate to Judaism is very limited, so it is the smallest of all world religions. Because the Jews are the chosen of God (Deuteronomy 7:6), the Jewish leadership rightly see their position on earth as representatives of God. They hold most strongly to retaining knowledge of Tanakh, but also to not breaking these laws, an earnest, no-nonsense moral code.

Second, the Christian religion believes Jesus is the Messiah who came and lived on earth without sin, or in other words, He obeyed the voice of God by not breaking the commandments of God. In doing so Jesus redeemed the world of the curse brought on the earth by Adam's disobedience. Jesus' death on the cross sealed the agreement to restore communication with God through the intercessor, the "go-between" (1 John 2:1; Hebrews 1:3, 13; Jesus Christ is at God's right hand). Now man no more must feel the need to hide from God ("And they [the people] said to Moses, speak thou to us, and we will hear; but let not God speak to us, lest we die." [Genesis 3:8, 10; Exodus 20:18–22]). Now the sin-free blood of Christ on the cross covers our inability to live by the law infallibly.

The first disciples of Christ knew the old Jewish book, the Tanakh. When Christ died (John 18:28) during the Jewish festival of Passover and came back from the grave three days later (Luke 24:7), the original disciples of Christ still lacked the confidence to do the acts of Christ, as Jesus stated they would in John 14:12, "He that believeth on me, the works that I do shall he do also; and greater works than these shall he do, because I go unto my Father." Also, Jesus told them (Luke 24:49) to stay in Jerusalem till He clothed them with power from on high. So on the fiftieth day of Passover, called by the Jews the Feast of Weeks, the Holy Spirit was sent from heaven to empower the original disciples of Christ with the second witness from heaven, which testifies or agrees to the known Word of God and gives direction to a life (Acts 2:1).

Now, at this point in time, the power of Christ could work in the disciples. Their duty was to spread the good news of God's mercy to all people on earth (Acts 1:8; Matthew 28:19; Mark 16:15; Luke 24:47). The Roman Empire controlled the known world at that time, and Paul, the converted Jewish Pharisee, brought testimony of Jesus Christ to Rome (Acts 23:11), the seat of that empire. It seemed evident that

Christians could expect the returning Messiah to rule the world. This is what they all had expected Jesus to do. It's what the disciples of John the Baptist spoke of to Jesus in Matthew 11:3 and it's what the Jews believe today will happen at the coming of Messiah. The fulfillment of all things is the presenting to all nations and people in the world the promise of redemption for their sins, in other words, restoration of the ability to fellowship with God (1 John 1:3). After the death of John, the last of the original disciples, around A.D. 95, the power of God working in the people appeared to decline, but after enduring centuries of much persecution, Christianity was made the state religion of the empire of Rome. In A.D. 313, Emperor Constantine made Christianity accepted in the Roman Empire by the Edict of Milan, and in A.D. 323 Christianity became the state religion, known as Catholicism. The Bible states clearly that the original disciples' knowledge of the Tanakh, the Old Testament, and their knowing of Jesus Christ was not sufficient power to overcome the fear of persecution and death (John 20:19). It also states the need of the power from on high, the Holy Ghost, to finish the work of God on earth (Luke 24:49). So it is perceivable by the written Word, by history and by experience that the written Word of God needed to be spread throughout the world. It then had to be translated into common language so that every person in every nation (whose leaders would allow it) would have the ability to make the free choice to follow God's command in their life.

The limit in Christianity today is the lack of personal knowledge of the written Word of God, so that individual identification of the Spirit of God cannot be proven (1 John 4:1). Without the dual evidence of this proof of God the population is easily deceived, but where two or more witnesses are in agreement, truth is known and direction is perceived by a more sure faith.

Third, the Muslim religion, brought about by their prophet Muhammad, was started around A.D. 610. They believe they worship the true God. At that time, the Jews were being dispersed throughout the world since their second temple was destroyed in A.D. 70. Also, Christianity was in decline since knowledge of the written Word of God was limited to the Catholic priests. Further, common people were generally unable to read, and Bibles were rare because of the expense and time involved in reproducing them by hand, until the invention of the printing press around A.D. 1445.

So, at that time the examples of biblical worship were either by a disheartened dispersed Jew who didn't readily accept converts, or the Christians of Rome who would persecute you if you didn't convert to Christianity in the form of the Catholic Church. The Muslim religion has its own set of rules that must be followed or violence is used to force subjection. It seems like the greatest use people made of this religion that traces its roots back to Abraham is its great power in the motivation of fear through violence. This is especially seen in the world today. We can hope that this motivation of fear will cause people to seek to know God through the written Word, and then prayerfully seek the direction of God, additionally utilizing our recorded history to come to a full understanding of God's desire for His creation, that is, fellowship in the light (1 John 1:7).

So, the fulfillment of all things is for all who willingly accept the invitation from God to read and study His Word, utilizing the insight and incitation of the Spirit of God (Ephesians 4:21; John 14:26; 1 John 2:20). Then each believer can go on to learn from God through Jesus Christ, by the Holy Ghost. Each one can bypass the deception of man and the corruption of our own flesh, removing ignorance and renewing the mind to the order of original intent. Thus the Holy Spirit gives incite, meaning the urge to action, leading to insight, meaning the ability to see God's way.

Let the peace in your heart be the indication of correct instruction (Colossians 3:15), learning how to know, hear, and obey your Father in heaven for perfect direction on earth. In reality, life in eternity, in heaven, means to desire to be with God, to please Him (Isaiah 53:10). So if we learn to know Him we can begin our life in eternity with Him today, right now. A pretty cool thought, that I believe is true.

EVIL CANNOT BE APPEASED

One of the definitions of the word "evil" used most of the time in the Old Testament comes from a primary Hebrew word which means to spoil, to break in pieces, to make good for nothing. To think that what is evil has any possibility of coexisting and accomplishing anything good and productive is an oxymoron. The main duty of evil in this system on God's earth seems to be a resistance to good for the purpose of making the believers stronger in their faith in God. Evil cannot be killed out of existence; it is a spirit and simply deceives its next victim.

However, evil is relentless and never quits its pursuit of dominance. The paradox of the battle between good and evil appears to be that when good gains power it seems to lose the desire to fight to restrain evil, postulating the idea that a compromise can be reached. This always results in good being dethroned and the council of death and destruction controlling the people.

So, what's the point? Perhaps history can show us the results of these evidences. History presents the record that good people gain control by turning their ways to the Word of God, but as good begins to compromise with evil it weakens its stronghold on the power of God and is overcome. At this low point believers are scattered by threat of violence and depart to another country and rebuild their relationship with God. Although believers suffer losses it is not without gaining better understanding of God's purpose in the earth. The obvious problem today is that there is no other country to run to and evil has fantastic ability to control. This leaves believers with only one option: that is to look up to heaven and into the Word of God to learn the final lesson before the return of Jesus Christ to punish the disobedient. That final lesson is to learn how to trust the Father in heaven to lead just as Jesus was led when He walked the earth. Our example as never before is Jesus Christ.

When Jesus walked the earth for thirty-three years, His main priority was to obey His Father in heaven and fulfill what was written in the Scriptures about Him. He even stated when being questioned by Pilate on the day that He would be crucified that, "If my kingdom were of this world then would my servants fight ... but now is my kingdom not from hence" (John 18:36). There is a time coming when Jesus will return with His servants and there will be a battle on earth for this kingdom (Revelation 14:1, 19:11–21). For now, our purpose on earth is to know God, by knowing His Word, to hear His voice and obey, and to fearlessly stand in resistance to evil.

That doesn't mean we kill every instance of evil that is perceived, or we would all have to kill each other. Also, history submits the proof in the book of Judges (21:25, 17:6), in the Bible, that even the Jews who were the best at keeping the Law of God couldn't overcome the steady growth of evil which always seeks to destroy. Also, the flood in which Noah was saved could not kill all evil. So we resist evil, not without violence, but steadily looking to God for our direction, knowing that our battle is not for the kingdom of this world. For now our battle is to seek the kingdom of God within us (Luke 17:21). So Christ is the Word of God written down by men of old as they by faith believed they heard His voice. So many years and lives have been spent to give us this ability, and today our obligation as believers is to read and know the

Word of God, the Bible. We must write the Word upon our heart as God impresses it upon us. Then seek to know His voice, recognize when God's Holy Spirit commands us, and obey. "We walk by faith not by sight" (2 Corinthians 5:7). "For we are saved by hope ... we do with patience...wait for that we see not" (Romans 8:24–25). Our greatest hope and promise is to discern God's direction from heaven for our daily lives, and also the return of Jesus Christ to reign on earth, our salvation.

Evil is simply disobedience to God. So when God's Law is defined by what the Bible says, a nation can be considered evil if its laws don't conform to the laws or principles written in the Bible. So in the earth at this time, the USA is surrounded by a world of evil. Also, our nation itself is enduring a battle between good and evil, dividing America over mindsets that are difficult to comprehend. In fact, hearing and seeing these issues debated on public media has revealed that the problems cannot be debated in sensible ways, exposing the key of confusion underlying the controversies. One evidence of evil is confusion. Confusion only dominates a nation when the leaders of both the church and the nation are themselves confused. Looking at the history of nations that have been affected by the Christian church entering their country, we see a pattern. The usual effect is initially very positive, then turns lukewarm, then at the end very cold. At the end of an era, some church leaders will join with the rulers of the nation to force the people into subjection to their authority, the supreme authority of men, rather than exemplifying how to know the Bible, grow in trust, and be in subjection to the Father of creation (Psalm 2:2–3). The usual conclusion of the pattern is a very restrictive ruling class that turns the masses of people against any person or group with a differing viewpoint. The end result is that people who believe God is pointing to an evolved understanding of His purpose are forced to leave their home and scatter to other places. Here is a brief chronological summary of this progression in a few nations, starting with the Jewish disciples of Jesus in Jerusalem (Acts 1:4). The first church of Jesus Christ did many great works of God in Jerusalem and the church grew (Acts 2:41, 4:4). The leaders of the church in Israel pointed people to trust in Jesus for forgiveness of sin (Acts 5:31–32). After about thirty years the persecution became so great in Israel that the believers were scattered out to the world (Acts 11:19, 22:18, 21–22, 23:11, 26:32, 28:16).

The Apostle Paul quoted the prophet Isaiah. In Acts 28:25–27 Paul expressed God's purpose at that time, about A.D. 60. He wrote that the majority of his people, the Jews, would have their eyes closed for a period of time, as is written in the book of the prophet Isaiah (Isaiah 6:9–10, 29:10–18, 44:18). The next nation spoken of in the Bible where a strong Christian church presence was mentioned is in the country that we call Turkey. That nation was the location of all the seven churches spoken of in the book of Revelation (Revelation 1:11, 2:1, 8, 12, 18, 3:1, 7, 14). Today the population of Turkey is ninety-eight percent Muslim (www.allaboutturkey.com). At about A.D. 380 Theodosius I, the last

Roman emperor to rule over both the eastern and western Roman Empire, declared Christianity the state religion. After his reign the area was divided and ruled by two Roman emperors. In A.D. 1054 the state church split into the Eastern Church called the Greek Orthodox Church and the Western called the Roman Catholic Church. After that, basically the dominant Christian religion in Western Europe was the Catholic Church and the dominant Christian religion in Eastern Europe was the Greek or Eastern Orthodox Church. At first glance these conflicts may bring to mind the many wars fought by these nations against each other.

After closer consideration, though, we can find that both after the death and the pain incurred in war and after the havoc wrought by church splits something new can emerge. There will be a few leaders who search deeper into the Bible to see what God intends. After experiencing the end of the destruction, they realize that man cannot accomplish the liberation of the human spirit by natural means. In accordance with this insight, they further investigate the Bible to understand the purpose of God on earth. This in turn has caused the Bible to be brought to every continent on earth and translated into the common language. So it is apparent that one of the most important elements of the Christian faith, the written Word of God, the Bible, has been transported to the people through these harrowing events. This gives even greater weight to the importance of the Bible in God's grand plan.

ALL THINGS ARE FULFILLED

This brings us fairly well to our world today. The issue is the same; man can't find a natural answer to the world's numerous problems and diminishes the importance of the knowledge of God. He becomes ignorant of the purpose of God, and so is transformed exponentially into deeper and darker evil.

The Bible says because of the darkening of their heart the people become past feeling and give themselves over to uncleanness with greediness (Ephesians 4:18–19).

In conclusion, history shows that the battle is for human souls. It is a battle where evil deceives mankind into killing each other for an unattainable peace and safety. At the same time God is wooing mankind to transform themselves by His Word and the leading of the Holy Spirit, ultimately changing them by faith into the image of His Son (Romans 8:29) to live by faith and patience, trusting in Him. You know, most people already do this—they live by faith; the common expression is "I'm going with my gut feeling." When you have the knowledge of the Bible combined with practice discerning the voice of the Holy Ghost, you simply go with the "God feeling."

There is a preparation going on, to desire life with God for eternity, to choose life with God more than things on earth, a free choice.

WHEN THE JEW AND THE GENTILE HAVE THEIR EYES OPEN

The fulfillment of all things is when the Jew looks at what the Christian is doing and saying and these actions of the Christian bear witness to the Jew's knowledge of the Word of God.

Right now the primary reason the Jew does not give preference to the Gentile religion of Jesus Christ is that the Christian mostly does not obey or keep knowledge of the law of God, and the Jew is all about honoring the law of God. There is another reason that Jews do not view the Christian religion as kosher. The Jew knows that the Lord thy God is one Lord (Deuteronomy 6:4), and since the typical Christian does not know the Word of God, they can't explain how there can be a Father, Son, and Holy Ghost, and yet they are one. The majority of Christians don't understand the relationship or the reasoning behind there being a Father, Son, and Holy Ghost in Christianity, so they can't give a viable explanation. This causes the Jew to dismiss Christianity altogether.

Yet, when the Christian is seen obeying the voice of God, according to the written Word, not just doing supernatural signs and wonders, then the whole plan of God will become visible. It will be plain to see and God will open eyes.

To understand the Trinity, perhaps the simplest example on earth of a model of one God in three forms might be the system of the government in the United States, regarding the way the president works in the executive branch. The president is the head; by his voice he makes decisions, then his decisions are carried out by ambassadors that he chooses. So it is with what is commonly called the Trinity, meaning the Father, Son, and Holy Spirit. The Father is the head; he sets all rules. His voice is the Spirit of God and His only begotten Son, Jesus, whom God trusted by faith, ("who first trusted in Christ" [Ephesians 1:12]; "waiting for the revealing, the revelation of the sons of God" [Romans 8:19]). God trusted with the hope that Jesus would be obedient to the voice of the Holy Spirit and the written Word, accomplishing the Father's will on earth, righting the wrong done by Adam, redeeming the sin Adam brought on the earth, by sacrificing His sin-free life for all the world.

You see, the Jewish religion already teaches a two-in-one God, because they know that the Father God in heaven doesn't lie. He doesn't change. He doesn't have to; He made all things. Yet their forefathers heard the voice of God by faith and wrote down the spoken Word of God which cannot be broken. So what the religion of Judaism is saying in essence is that they worship the Father in heaven and they worship the written Word of God on earth, a dual God. In fact, the Jew will say that they are of the seed of their father Abraham. Yet Abraham was not born of a virgin, so he carried the corrupted seed of Adam from both his father and mother. We see that the standard golden rule of Judaism and Christianity, written in Deuteronomy 6:4–6 and Matthew 22:36–38, is still not seen and understood in its fullest form. Obedience to the Father in heaven is our greatest goal on earth. Jesus' purpose was to give us the most uncorrupted access to God's throne in heaven. So through Jesus we now have the confirming witness of the Holy Spirit dwelling in us believers. His presence gives testimony to the <u>uncorrupted</u> Word of God written upon our heart, that the objective of obedience might be fulfilled in us who believe. This will only be fully accomplished by the labor of loving God with all your heart, soul, and mind by knowing His written Word.

CHAPTER 3

THE VOICE

BRAINWASHING BY FAMILIAR SPIRIT

GOD'S DESIRE IS FOR US to hear His voice, by faith, from heaven, and obey. Satan's job is to deceive us to believe his lying tall tales. God's desire is obedience, not just fearful obedience, but obedience out of our love for the Father and hatred for evil. All decisions come down to faith or fear. So the battle is accurately knowing and discerning the voice of God from His temple in heaven. His testimony, His witness. The devil's plan really is simple, that is to mix up God's words, confuse them. Then the devil simply replaces God's truth with Satan's lying words, then ingrains his lies in our mind, developing his bad habits in us, trying to cover up the life of God in our heart. But Psalm 19:3 says that all people hear His voice. So our approach for gaining firm direction is to know the Bible so that we can discern His voice proceeding from the temple in heaven by comparing to the written truth we know.

But here is the punch line; here is the "cool" thing. Right now on earth we have the most sure way to get clear direction, and it is by this labor of knowing His Word (Hebrews 4:11) and discerning His voice (Hebrews 5:14) by faith. The testimony comes from the temple of God in heaven, so if we willingly seek to know our Father diligently now, then we get to hear from His throne in heaven today and forever! (Revelation 22:14). There seems to be something deep and yet simple about this understanding!

BRAINWASHING

The term "brainwashing" is not heard much today, but it was commonly heard in the late 60s and early 70s when I was a young boy. It seemed like a scary mysterious thing and I wondered if a normal person could be fooled to believe a lie and be brainwashed. Usually the people being brainwashed were our men who were taken prisoner in war, not in everyday life.

Then one day shortly after I was touched by Jesus and knew that He was real, I was confronted by someone I loved dearly. This person told me that I was brainwashed because I was telling everyone about what Jesus did when He healed me, just by asking Him to do it. My response to my loved one was instant and unrehearsed. I said, "We are all brainwashed by something, why not by God?"

I spoke a truth and I didn't realize how foundational the truth was. For at that time I was brainwashed by the limited knowledge I had of God. It was enough to get me healed but not enough to lead me in my everyday decisions.

So, my dearly loved one was right. I was brainwashed, not completely by God, but by people who knew the truth of God. That bit of knowledge was enough to heal my body, so I was OK with being incomplete in knowledge of the Bible since even with just partial knowledge, I got healed! Faith in God's Word gave me back the ability to work and provide for my family.

As time went on, the lack of integrity in Christians around me began to really trouble me till I started reading the Bible myself and realized that every one of us has failed in some way to measure up to the law and perfection of God written in the Bible. "If we say we have not sinned, we make Him a liar, and His word is not in us"(1 John 1:10). This is the purpose of Jesus being sin-free; He obeyed God, even dying on the cross for the sins of the world. "And [Jesus] became obedient unto death" (Philippians 2:8). The Jews had a tradition that anyone who hung on a cross was cursed. So Jesus took the curse of the sins of the world on Himself by submitting to death on a cross. Our job now is to trust Jesus, know the law, remember our covenant with God (Psalm 103:18), do whatever He commands, as best we can, hear His voice and obey.

WHAT'S IN THE WORD FULFILLMENT?

Fulfillment is to hear from God through Jesus Christ for our direction on earth each day. It is very similar to going to work at a job each day, and to "clock in," or be on the job at a certain time. At some jobs we must see the boss or manager for direction for that day. At other times we simply go to our duty and if the boss needs to see us he will call for us or come visit us on the job. The end result is that we <u>know</u> what we are hired to do and we do it with excellence each day and get better at our job as we become more knowledgeable. This idea of knowing our job and being attentive to the boss' desire is how we fulfill our commitment with our Boss in heaven.

FAMILIAR SPIRITS

When a voice in your spirit gives supernatural knowledge, the fact of that knowledge does not prove that voice's loyalty to God or His Word. All supernatural acts of God should lead us to Him, giving a strong desire to know Him and communicate with Him. The action that the voice of a spirit directs us to and the Word of God must agree.

In doing a word study on "familiar spirit" I was very surprised to find that there was no Hebrew definition for the word "familiar." In order to understand in English what the meaning of the Hebrew word was, two English words were needed. The phrase "familiar spirit" is defined in a single Hebrew word for spirit. Here again was another surprise and wonderful understanding which gave great insight to discern the Spirit of God from the spirit of error. One of the words for spirit here means "prattling," meaning to chatter, babble, or just speaking words with no reason, foolishly, or sounding like air being blown over a bottle top.

The importance of discerning a familiar spirit is that if we can't discern, we may have given that voice notable worth and influence in our life by the conditioning of our surroundings. In other words, we may be impulsively obeying authority in our conscience that we have given a value higher than the guidelines of the Bible and we may not be aware of it. Possibly what we believe we were born with, our normal disposition, was just a deception conditioned in our mind by familiarity.

What a great awareness to know we can change ourselves for the better just by meditating on the written words of God. How wonderful that our natural persuasions could be changed to do what the Holy Spirit of God says. We can be conscious of our old familiar spirit and become more closely associated with the Spirit of God and know the comfort He brings. I can testify from my own experience that the transformation of God's peace is truly amazing! When I recognized the areas of my belief system that I believed were truth, but which opposed the Bible, I then worked to transform my foundational principles to what the Bible said was truth. It was like driving from New Jersey to Florida in the winter, from death to life! (The truth will make you free [John 8:32].).

Judaism

Jesus

Original Apostles in Jerusalem

Church of Roman Empire   Lutheran   Catholicism

Greek Orthodox Church   Anglican Church

Methodist Church   Presbyterian Church

Baptist Church   Congregational Church

Mennonite Church   Puritans   Pilgrims

Church of Christ   Advent Church

Latter Day Saints   Church of God

Assembly of God   Holiness Church

Foursquare Church   Word of Faith

Charismatic Movement

CHAPTER 4

THE LIMITS OF DENOMINATIONS

FOLLOW GOD OR FOLLOW MAN

I AWOKE THIS MORNING (8-5-18) on my bed with thoughts of what I have been taught by Jesus Christ, His Holy Spirit, and how many of those things disagree with my dear church family in Christian denominations. I believe that the Teacher instructed me to list these many differences between denominational teachings and Scripture, and to make a case for truth. I do this first for myself, and then for anyone interested.

I would also interject here a truth that I have found important for me personally, and I believe for any person seeking to know the direction of God. It is that fulfillment is hearing the voice of direction which comes from the throne of God in heaven through Jesus Christ. When a person starts out in this walk with God they need a human teacher. "How then shall they call on Him whom they have not believed?

And how shall they believe in Him of whom they have not heard? And how shall they hear without a preacher? ... So then faith cometh by hearing, and hearing by the word of God" (Romans 10:14, 17). But as their mind is opened by the Word of God and then transformed to the Word, it becomes engraved upon their heart, or in other words the seed of the Word is placed in the heart, then the voice of God instructs personally. In order to keep growing, a mature Christian must develop more confidence in God's personal leadings than in the limits set by God in men long ago in a denomination.

The best way I have found to comprehend this is to think of Christian truths through the years, which usually form new denominations sort of like schools of higher learning. As the truth is grasped, the church continues on the path the Lord leads, which is usually very stable, but not flexible to change. One of the greatest benefits we have at this time is our ability to look back at a great deal of church history and have a much better comprehensive view of what God is doing and how the serpent deceives. This should give the maturing Christian more understanding and insight to be able to endure and overcome. So here is a list of common Scriptures or understandings I have heard preached about which the Holy Spirit has taught further or differently as He brings them to mind, in Jesus' name.

    1. There is no personal interpretation of Scriptures but as men of old were led by the Holy Spirit (2 Peter 1:21). This in practicality is interpreted as meaning

that the leaders of the denomination must agree with you, or you with them. So, the Scripture says, "The Holy Ghost led men of old" (to new understanding), but in order to accept the teaching of the Holy Spirit today, the leaders of the denomination must see it also. So if they don't see it, how could you believe the Holy Ghost would speak to you and not to them? The truth is that the leaders have so much responsibility that at times they get caught up in the time constraints of their duties and simply fall back on the answer, "We always did it this way." It is an easy trap to fall into, not a fault, just the habitual nature of human behavior not to want to be alone with God. ("And the people said unto Moses, speak thou with us, and we will hear; but let not God speak to us, lest we die" [Exodus 20:19].)

2. Next, there is the great importance of knowing what God has revealed today through the book of Revelation so the church will understand what the war on earth is about and not get distracted by unnecessary and energy draining battles. There is a need to be definitive about the conclusion of the purpose of the book of Revelation in order to hear God correctly and develop a strategy designed by God for today's end-time saint, which simply is to know God, hear His voice, and obey.

3. Next is the teaching regarding "Where two or three or more witnesses agree is truth" (Hebrews 10:28). This Scripture means to some denominations that

the two witnesses are the Bible and the promises in the Bible. This is usually quoted along with "God is not a man that He should lie" (Numbers 23:19), and "All the promises are yea and amen" (2 Corinthians 1:20). Rather, it seems obvious that the two witnesses are the written Word of God and the living voice of God, the Holy Spirit. For this purpose a believer begins the labor to engrave the Word upon their heart to change from their old way of thinking. This develops more trust or confidence to believe the Holy Ghost is actually speaking to you. The key is that the living voice must agree with the written Word. The difficulty comes when God's voice conflicts with the standard belief in Christian denominations, that standard belief being that men need to be directed by men, when the goal of leaders should be developing a people confident in God's direction, by faith.

4. Also, there are false beliefs through corrupted understanding. One example of this would be a church teaching that God would not allow pain, when the Bible says otherwise: "Though He were a Son, yet learned He obedience by the things which He suffered" (Hebrews 5:8).

The false teaching is that God would never allow something bad to happen to us for any reason. The Bible clearly states repeatedly that God allows and uses this tactic quite effectively.

This false belief is rooted in the desire for God never to allow people to be in pain. However, the Bible states that God is developing overcomers to lead the people, who must endure great pains both now and at the end of the thousand year reign. Then they will rule and reign for eternity, and there will be no pains in eternity. This I believe is the primary issue with female leadership. The female was created by God to nurture, not to punish or to inflict harm. There seems to be a battle going on inside most women whenever violence is contemplated or if the suggestion is made that God could be involved in these acts of punishment or direction adjustment. Of course, most men are the opposite and look at violence as a way of proving a thing or person. So, a man needs the nurturing spirit of the woman to make the best possible decisions, but when the leaders are female, the idea of exercising power to influence conditions is usually fought "tooth and nail." A wise man would rather not subject a situation to violence except only as a last resort. It seems that by the time a woman reluctantly agrees to the way of force it may be too late to subdue the enemy.

5. Although in some Christian denominations prophets are accepted and welcomed, in practice it is much more accepted if the message from God through the prophet causes the people to clap and smile and rejoice. The Bible shows that the message from God

through the prophets was hated so much that prophets would hide out for their own safety. Jesus confirms this in Luke 13:34 and Matthew 23:37 by saying how often the prophets were killed by the religious leaders. The message from God to the people is many times a warning or rebuke. A message of this sort is not well received then or now. This is an indication that the will of the people dominates, not God's voice.

6. One of the most disturbing tendencies of some Christian denominations is to reference mass media outlets, magazines, books, radio, and often major Christian TV personalities to prove a point or emphasize a subject, especially when preaching or teaching. This is very disturbing, because what we reference as our source becomes our guide. Of course, if a person believes the Bible is a book written simply by the hand of man from his mind rather than inspired by God, by the Spirit of God, then this type of referencing is only natural and would be expected. The Bible tells us there is a new and better way to know God's desire for us. We read, know, then write the Word of God upon the heart. Then we develop and grow in our confidence and trust by faith to hear, recognize, and obey the voice of God which directs our life from the throne in heaven (Jeremiah 31:31–34). It seems our leaders always become more comfortable telling people what God says, rather than instructing the people to learn and receive from God and go out believing

He will lead, guide, and sustain them. This is especially critical in these last of the last days in which we live. When this nation falls, the religious leaders will be silenced, or better said, the leaders will be silenced from speaking the message from the Holy Spirit, the living voice of God from His throne in heaven. ("Let us therefore come boldly unto the throne of grace, where we may obtain mercy, and find grace to help in our time of need" [Hebrews 4:16].)

What these evidences make compellingly clear is that the authority in Christian denominations does not intend to follow where they can't see God leading. If "the shoe were on the other foot," I would agree with the institutions. Since I believe the Lord is leading by His command, blessed are they that do His commandments (Revelation 22:14). There must be obedience to what the living voice directs, so as the voice speaks within the framework of His written Word and principle, so a person does their best to obey.

Here then, concisely, are four statements of truth for these days that we are in:

1. The book of Revelation must be held and taught to its reasonable conclusion. That is that in the end the earth will be controlled by a demonically led headship, which, according to the Holy Bible, will violently remove freedom to worship God. This will mean destruction of all references to the truth. People and material and believers will be here to show the power and mercy of God until the day of the hour of His wrath

which falls upon the disobedient (Revelation 18:4, 8, 10, 17; Revelation 9:20–21).

2. All Christians must have faith to believe they can hear and see the direction of God through Jesus Christ (the written Word) and the voice of the testimony, His agreeing witness (the Holy Spirit), in order to be led by truth in the way of the Lord. Jesus said, "The Son can do nothing of himself, but what He seeth the Father do." Also Jesus said, "I can of my own self do nothing; as I hear I judge ... because I seek not my own will, but the will of the Father which hath sent me" (John 5:19, 30, 12:44, 46, 14:17).

3. The purpose of these times is to prepare a people who can overcome the fear of these times in order to bring in the last of end-time harvest. This includes both the harvest of souls who simply hear and believe ("For whosoever shall call upon the name of the Lord shall be saved" [Romans 10:13]), and the development of overcoming saints who are being trained to rule and reign with God and Christ, the disciples of Christ (Revelation 5:10, 11:15, 20:6, 22:5).

4. Finally, I believe this last day movement of the Spirit of God will not be a new denomination. Like the first disciples and like our Lord Jesus Christ, we will be as special forces advisors, helping, leading, advising, and overcoming evil in the name of Jesus Christ until He returns, making our home church in the

denomination that the Lord leads us to, always obedient to the Lord's command.

MORE POINTS THAT SOME CHRISTIAN LEADERS TEACH CONTRARY

1. First, many churches teach that "keeping the Law" means to not break the Law, when the Bible teaches that we should remember the Law if we love Jesus. "If a man loves me [Jesus] he will keep my words" (John 14:23). The truth about this must fit the definition of the word "keep" and fit the Bible truth that we do sin, ("If we say we have not sinned, we make Him [God] a liar, and His word is not in us" [1 John 1:10]). To keep the Law means we retain knowledge of the Law, and we memorize the Word, because we are creatures of habit. When we have put the Word of God in our heart we are more likely to do it.

2. Next, we are told by leaders that we must be an example of never sinning in order to bring people to faith in Christ, when the Bible tells us all have sinned and come short of God (Romans 3:23). The Word of God tells us that we should labor to know the Bible (Jesus is the Word: Hebrews 4:11; John 1:1) so that we can recognize His voice and obey. It is obedience to the command of God that draws others to our God. His timing is perfect. We can't be perfect; we try, fail, forgive, and show and accept mercy and live life in

Christ. We retain the Word of God, we know it, just like anybody that does a job, or an athlete on a team knows how to do their job. Everybody makes mistakes on a job. The purpose is to obey the Boss, overcome mistakes, and carry on. Perfection is in Him. This is a way that draws a person to Christ. ("A word spoken in due season, how sweet it is!" [Proverbs 15:23]).

3. Some leaders teach that a confession of faith in Christ does not mean you are saved, that is, that you are going to heaven, but that you need a relationship with Jesus. So how do you define relationship? Jesus says what we do is believe He was sent by God, by faith (John 5:24), then when we are so led, read and study the Word, and pray to know Jesus (the Word). We are saved when we believe Christ died for our sin, then we grow in knowledge and confidence in Him. Of course, this is where families become so important. Mom and Dad are teaching the children, and the parents and children are growing in the knowledge of the Lord as they study the Word to understand. The crucial point is that they teach obedience to God first, by knowing the Word and then recognizing the Spirit, first proving (1 John 4:1), and after recognizing God's voice (Romans 12:2), obeying His direction.

4. Sometimes we are told to be "fruit inspectors" in order to know we are following the Lord and that others are following the Lord also, when the Bible tells us to follow Christ and obey God's voice, the Holy Ghost.

When we become overly concerned with what people think of us we are in danger of becoming people pleasers, not God followers. We are not to be led by what we produce, our fruit; we are to be led by faith that we hear the voice of God as it agrees with the Bible and/or its principles. Using Jesus as our example, how many times did His disciples agree with what God told Him to do? Fulfillment is to obey God's voice.

Herein lies the problem. The devil works his lies that seem like truth because they contain partial truth. You see, it is pretty easy for adults to recognize when people are following people and it doesn't persuade them toward Christ and belief in God. This may also be a reason the Bible tells us God desires to scatter the power of the holy people and then the end will come (Daniel 12:7). For when people follow people they become an identified group, a denomination. But when people follow the person of Jesus Christ they become identified by His character and point others to His truth, to faith in God through Jesus Christ. Possibly, better put, the best example is us in the Word, the written Word of God, the Bible, which is the spoken voice of God written as the writers of the Bible heard the voice of God, by faith. Then as the Word is engraved upon our heart, it's in us. Then we recognize the living voice of God speaking to us this day, then act and do by faith what God is directing us from heaven's throne. We become one in God, in Christ, as Jesus was when He walked the earth. Consider Jesus' prayer, "Sanctify them through thy truth: Thy word is truth" (John 17:17).

THE SPIRIT OF SCORNED WOMEN IN AUTHORITY

The head of the evil coalition spoken of in Revelation 17:3, known as the woman who sits upon the seat (of authority) of the beast, is actually not an individual. In Revelation 17:18 she is described as, "that great city which reigns over the kings of the earth." This city will have the spirit of a woman scorned. The anger of this head will be deflected and deceived by the serpent, the devil, who is the source of all evil, and will be focused upon men; the head of the evil coalition will become the pawn of the devil. The anger of the scorned woman towards man will be the enmity God intended to be between the woman and the serpent. ("And I will put enmity between thee [the serpent] and the woman, and between thy seed and her seed" [Genesis 3:15].) The woman is again being deceived by the devil because the majority of men have never had or else have lost their knowledge of the Bible. They no longer discern the voice of the Spirit of God; they are inexperienced at relying on God's guidance. For this reason most men are no longer led by the Spirit of God from heaven and they have become ineffective against darkness and the plans of the devil, which leaves the woman an easy prey of Satan. The Bible tells us that if the church is not subject to Christ, neither is the wife obligated to submit to her husband. So godly men and husbands are a key component to the whole system of the church functioning at its highest level. This same passage of Scripture in the book of Ephesians informs us that this is accomplished by the washing, the cleansing, and sanctifying of the church by the Word of God. Like a computer, what we are programmed by is how we will respond (Ephesians 5:21–27).

When you see evidence of this in earth, especially in positions of authority, you will know the time of the end is very near.

STEPS OF CHURCH PERFECTION

The fulfillment of the church in the earth will be when all the world will know the purpose of God sending Jesus Christ and starting the church. Today many Christians will say, "I go to church, so I am a Christian." That is good, but not the best. A second person will say, "I am a Christian for I have made a confession that Jesus died for my sin." That is good, but not the best. A third group will say, "I have asked Jesus to come into my heart and rule my life. I am a born-again Christian." That is better, but not the best. A fourth person will say, "I have read the Bible; I am a Christian." That is better, but not the best. A fifth group will say, "I have asked Jesus to rule my life and not only have I read the Bible, but I have memorized parts that He has told me. I am all I can be in Christ." That is perfect, but not all. The fulfillment of all things in Christ is to be full of God's Word, the Bible, then to recognize the voice of the Holy Spirit of God, so that you live and grow in trust in Him, because you love Him so much that you continuously fill yourself with Him. Then you hear His living command from the throne of God in heaven through Jesus Christ (the intercessor) and you "act now" on His royal command to you. You "come quickly," you "act now" on His command because you have continually removed every place that the corrupted information from the serpent has been used to resist the pleasure (Isaiah 53:10) of the Power of God working through you to accomplish the perfect will of our Father in heaven.

So ask Jesus to come into your heart and life and take over governance, or maybe better said, oversight. Read the Bible and memorize the parts that pertain to your life. Then practice recognizing His voice and acting on His direction, learning to live by the faith of God and to not depend on or be fearful of man.

WHEN HE SCATTERS THE POWER, IT IS FINISHED

I heard it said today on TV that history is damned to repeat itself. I have heard this saying as far back as I can remember. It always seems to emphasize the evil deeds that recur, but if we look at the development of Christianity through the ages we see an increased understanding of God's purpose as His knowledge is spread throughout the earth. This repetition is largely due to evil repeating itself in an effort to control or stop the Word of God in the earth, but the result of the evil attack causes an increased hunger for those seeking to understand more fully God's purpose in mankind on the earth. As Christians are scattered further around the globe they are forced by necessity to seek God for their protection and provision. It is written in the book of Daniel:

"When I have accomplished the scattering of the power of the holy people, all these things shall be finished [or fulfilled]" (Daniel 12:7).

As evil increases its control over God's people, because there is nowhere else to run for safety or to spread God's Word, we will be drawn to Him across the earth as never before. At this time the cry of the people for Christ's return will fill the heavens.

CONCLUSION

THE LORD SAID "WRITE A Conclusion to *All Things Are Fulfilled*. In it tell the people that this is what God wants to do for you also. Tell them of the adventure!! How God wants to bring them into places that only He knows. He wants them to be fulfilled, as only they were meant to be, for His pleasure to be done in their life (Isaiah 53:10)." Jesus said, "I only do what pleases the Father and He that sent me is with me; the Father hath not left me alone, for I do always those things that please him" (John 8:29). In that life is the greatest reward and the greatest adventure. For me it took many years and decades to realize that to know the Bible is to know the voice of God, but for you, with these insights, understanding God's desire for your life, there is no telling how quickly He will act and what awaits you. He had to tell me in 1996 that I would need to write. Then the Lord directed, "Write all that I have shown you about the book of Revelation."

That took five years, from 2009-2014. Afterward I found almost nobody was interested about what I believed God showed me about the book of Revelation, but the writing of the book gave me satisfaction. Then the Lord said in 2015, after a layoff from memorizing of about ten years, to start memorizing again. After about a year of memorizing, He said that I should write a simple short narrative of each chapter of the book of Revelation with a summary and conclusion. That book took a little over two years to complete, from 2015 to 2018, but I didn't sense the Lord wanting me to try to get people to read it. Then the same month I was finishing the second book, in February 2018, the Lord said, "This third book will be called *All Things Are Fulfilled*." This book was written in an inspirational fashion, meaning as the Lord would speak during my workday or as I was sleeping. I would stop or get up in the night and write what He said to me. It is very exciting! So, at the end of this third book, the Holy Spirit began to show me how the three books would actually be a series, or trilogy. Not just to reveal what the final purpose of the book of Revelation is, but to demonstrate to all how they also could see how God wants them to know their full purpose for Him, by hearing His direction.

So take the initiative, and develop your focus more singly on the Lord (Matthew 6:22). Focus on His Word and "hear" and "see" what He has intended for your life (John 5:19, 30).

Truly, life in Christ, in the Word, and the Spirit is God's desire for His people. Become His son or daughter and enjoy life as never before! (John 1:12).

Finally, at this time in America, there seems to be a strong contradiction about what it means to be a Christian. The Bible tells us we should love one another. Jesus said in John

13:34–35, "A new commandment I give unto you, that you love one another; as I have loved you, that you also love one another. By this shall all men know that ye are disciples, if you have love one to another." With this being understood it seems obvious that Christians do not even love all the members of their own church, let alone those that attend a different church or denomination, or the sinners who don't call themselves Christians. How can this be? In another place in the Bible, where Jesus is speaking of the last of the last days on earth, Jesus says "whoso readeth the book of Daniel [Matthew 24:15], let him understand." In this book of Daniel a question is answered about when the end of all things will be. The messenger of God tells Daniel in chapter 12, verse 7, "When he [God] shall have accomplished to scatter the power of the holy people, all these things shall be finished." So why or how could God expect us to love one another when the forces of the world continue to come against the Christians, causing us to scatter for our own safety? Let me give an illustration of unity from an experience I had that I believe gives the answer and the reason or purpose of our Lord scattering us to be alone with Him. To love Him is to know His Word (John 14:23).

In the mid and late 90s I attended a few Christian men's meetings which were called "Promise Keepers." In these meetings they did something that I had never before encountered and I was amazed at the sensation of unity that I experienced. In these meetings there were thousands of men and at a point in the meeting the speaker would tell us men to shout out the name of the church we attended. The sound was unrecognizable noise. Then the speaker said to shout out the name of the one who saved your soul. In one voice, in one name, there was the absolute recognition of the unifying name of Jesus! It was stunning. I couldn't imagine what that would be like; it had to be experienced in order to know it. Unity is in Jesus, so to know Jesus is unity, since Jesus is the Word. When we know the Bible, we are one, having unity in Him. This is what this book, *All Things Are Fulfilled*, goes into depth expounding on, the simplicity of unity that is right before our eyes. That is, to have unity is to know the Bible (John 14:23), to read it over and over until it becomes our way of thinking. Then when we hear His voice speaking to us we will recognize Him. Since Jesus said He only does what He hears and sees the Father doing (John 5:19, 30), we can be assured we are in unity with the only one and true God, because the Bible says in John 1:1, 14 that "Jesus is the Word," and the Word is the breath of God, His Spirit. Our confidence and trust in God grows as His Spirit teaches us what we didn't know and we continue to keep reinforcing the words of the Bible in our heart. Our unity comes as we become one in God, unified by Christ.

So the end of it all is that unity comes when individual believers know, hear, and obey the voice of God from heaven. Unity comes through obedience to the living voice of God in heaven directing our lives on earth, confirmed to us by knowledge of His written Word. True unity is oneness with God, through the sacrifice of His only begotten Son,

Jesus. His sin-free blood covers our inadequacies. Unity comes by faith in Him, controlled not by men, but by trust and confidence in His truth. We are in unity with God's people, including the Host of Heaven (Psalm 103:19, 21). Unity is being controlled as Jesus is, only by the command of our Father in heaven, not by men.

If you enjoyed this book, will you help me spread the word?

THERE ARE SEVERAL WAYS YOU can help me get the word out about the message of this book…

- Post a 5–Star review on Amazon.
- Write about the book on your Facebook, Twitter, Instagram, LinkedIn—any social media you regularly use!
- If you blog, consider referencing the book, or publishing an excerpt from the book with a link back to my Amazon listing. You have my permission to do this as long as you provide proper credit and backlinks.
- Recommend the book to friends—word-of-mouth is still the most effective form of advertising.
- Purchase additional copies to give away as gifts.

Contact me by email at nfcc@windstream.net.